Developing Executive Functioning
in the Primary Years

Developing Executive Functioning
in the Primary Years
SOWATT CAN WE DO TO EMPOWER LEARNERS?

Dr Rosalyn Muir

To Lorna and Katherine, who continue to teach me as much about life and learning as any classroom ever could.

Copyright © Rosalyn Muir 2026

All rights reserved. No part of this book may be reproduced or transmitted in any form or by any means, electronic or mechanical, including photocopying, recording or by any information storage and retrieval system, without prior permission in writing from the publisher.

Published by Amba Press
Melbourne, Australia
www.ambapress.com.au

Editor – Rica Dearman
Cover Designer – Tess McCabe

ISBN: 9781923403369 (pbk)
ISBN: 9781923403376 (ebk)

A catalogue record for this book is available from the National Library of Australia.

Contents

Foreword	1
Introduction: Preparing students for lifelong learning	3
Chapter 1: Inside the learning brain	13
Chapter 2: Introducing the SOWATT approach	21
Chapter 3: Self-regulation	45
Chapter 4: Organisation	55
Chapter 5: Working memory	69
Chapter 6: Attention	81
Chapter 7: Thinking flexibly	93
Chapter 8: Thinking about thinking	101
Chapter 9: Unpacking the curriculum through the SOWATT lens	117
Chapter 10: Getting started	135
References	145
Acknowledgements	152
About the author	153
Resources	155

Foreword

In every classroom, teachers witness moments that reveal something extraordinary about learning. A child pauses before rushing into a task, takes a breath and tries a new strategy. Another catches their own mistake, rereads a problem and corrects it. These small moments are not accidents – they are expressions of the developing executive functions that help children navigate their thinking, emotions and actions.

As educators, we often talk about helping students 'learn how to learn'. Yet, this simple phrase captures one of the most complex and vital processes in education. It is the foundation of self-regulated learning – the ability to plan, monitor and evaluate one's learning with purpose and adaptability. Executive functions form the cognitive engine that drives this process. They allow students to hold goals in mind, resist distractions and shift between ideas – all essential to navigating the challenges of modern learning.

What Dr Rosalyn Muir has done in *Developing Executive Functions in the Primary Years* is to illuminate the often unseen processes of learning – and show how they can be taught and nurtured. Drawing on research studies and classroom experience, she offers practical ways for teachers to intentionally teach these skills from the earliest primary years. This book honours the reality that executive functions are not fixed traits but can be shaped through the routines, questions and environments we create for our young people.

For educators reading this, please know that your role is pivotal. Every prompt you give, every moment of guided reflection and every invitation for students to think about their own thinking builds the foundation for lifelong learning. When children learn to direct their attention, manage their emotions and adjust their strategies, they not only improve their academic outcomes – they begin to form an important identity, that of a capable learner.

It's a privilege to introduce a book that aligns so deeply with this vision. My hope is that, as you read, you will not only find practical strategies to use tomorrow, but also the courage to centre what matters most – empowering learners for lifelong success.

Dr Shyam Barr
Author of *Educate to Self-Regulate:*
Empowering Learners for Lifelong Success
Adjunct Associate Professor, University of Canberra

Introduction

Preparing students for lifelong learning

> *"Learning is a continuous process of self-renewal, expanding our capabilities and our understanding of the world"*
> – Peter Senge

We are living in an era of rapid global change. Our media reflects the uncertainty through fragmented narratives, heightened polarisation and an overwhelming flow of information that often blurs the line between truth and perception. Traditionally, education systems have aimed to prepare students for the workforce and contributing to communities in the future, yet no one can say with any certainty what that future is going to look like. Several global institutions, including the World Economic Forum (WEF, 2025) and the Organisation for Economic Co-operation and Development (OECD, 2025) have, nevertheless, taken some steps to identify the key skills they believe will be necessary for success in an evolving job market. According to the latest *Future of Jobs Report* (WEF, 2025), the top 10 most valued skills will be:

1. Analytical thinking
2. Resilience, flexibility and agility
3. Leadership and social influence

4. Creative thinking
5. Motivation and self-awareness
6. Technological literacy
7. Empathy and active listening
8. Curiosity and lifelong learning
9. Talent management
10. Service orientation and customer service

This raises the question: What does this mean for schools? How are educational systems intentionally fostering these skills to ensure that students are equipped to meet the challenges of tomorrow?

One way education systems are responding to this uncertain and rapidly evolving landscape is by designing curriculum frameworks that emphasise not only academic achievement, but also personal growth, global competences and social responsibility. This shift is clearly reflected in the stated goals and priorities of education departments across many developed countries. To illustrate this, take a look at the following:

- **Australia:** The national curriculum aims to "help all young Australians to become successful learners, confident and creative individuals, and active and informed citizens" (Australian Curriculum, Assessment and Reporting Authority, ACARA, n.d.).
- **Canada:** Educational goals include fostering competencies: collaboration, creativity, social responsibility, global understanding and critical thinking, and aims to "ensure inclusive and quality education for all and promote lifelong learning" (Government of Canada, n.d.).
- **England:** The national curriculum introduces students to essential knowledge and helps them appreciate human creativity and achievement, fostering responsible citizenship (Department for Education, UK, n.d.).
- **Finland:** The objective of basic education is to support pupils' growth as ethically responsible members of society, providing the knowledge and skills necessary for life (Ministry of Education and Culture, Finland, n.d.).

- **New Zealand:** The education system aims to help students reach their full potential, develop resilience and become confident, creative and critical thinkers, while valuing cultural diversity and encouraging initiative (Ministry of Education, New Zealand, n.d.).
- **USA:** Educational objectives focus on promoting student achievement and preparing individuals for global competitiveness, ensuring equal access to educational opportunities (U.S. Department of Education, n.d.).

While many of these curriculum goals reflect an inspiring vision for holistic, future-focused education, the reality within classrooms often falls short of these ambitions. Despite policy-level commitments to personal growth, creativity and global citizenship, day-to-day teaching is frequently dominated by standardised testing, rigid accountability measures and overloaded curricula. Teachers are under pressure to cover large amounts of content in a limited time, leaving little room to cultivate the deeper competencies described in national frameworks. In practice, the gap between what education systems *aspire to* and what they *deliver* can be significant, especially in under-resourced schools, where constraints around time, training and support make it difficult to prioritise anything beyond basic academic outcomes.

Unfortunately, education is notorious for its cyclical trends and fads, with policymakers frequently promoting 'new' teaching methods that are often superseded a few years later. Even so-called 'evidence-based' approaches are not immune to this cycle. Indeed, I have witnessed and fallen victim to them myself during my career. If students are truly going to be able to respond to the unknown challenges, it can be argued that they need to be taught and supported *to learn how to learn*. Traditional education teaches us *what* to think, not *how* to think. All too often, we memorise facts for tests, then forget them. Teaching students *how* to learn is likely one of the most powerful tools for long-term success; it could even be considered the ultimate survival tool. Let's consider the reasons why:

- **Lifelong learning skills:** Knowledge and technology evolve rapidly. If students know *how* to learn, they can keep growing and adapting well beyond school, no matter what field they enter.

- **Independence and confidence:** Students who know how to learn are able to set goals, track their progress and reflect on outcomes. This kind of autonomy builds confidence and encourages a proactive mindset instead of waiting to be told what to do.
- **Resilience and adaptability:** When students can manage their own learning, they are better equipped to handle setbacks. They learn to see failure as feedback and an opportunity to learn, rather than defeat.
- **Improved academic performance:** Studies show that students who use strategies like planning, goal setting, time management and self-reflection tend to perform better academically (Zhai et al., 2023).
- **Critical thinking and metacognition:** Learning *how* to learn boosts metacognition – thinking about your thinking. This sharpens critical thinking and helps students approach challenges more strategically (Eberhart et al., 2025).
- **Transferable skills:** Knowing how to learn doesn't just apply to academics, it's useful in the workplace, in relationships and in personal development.

Learning *how* to learn has not previously received the priority and importance that it deserves, but times are changing and the chances are you are reading this book because you, too, have come to this important conclusion. The challenge is *how* to teach our students how to be better learners. I believe that one way to achieve this is by having a focus on the skills that research is clearly telling us underpin academic success and social-emotional wellbeing: **self-regulation and executive functions** (Moffit et al., 2011; Kitil et al., 2025). These are the skills that help students manage their emotions, organise their thoughts, prioritise tasks, resist the temptation to give in to distractions, solve problems and get tasks done on time. Their intentional development is often overlooked and, consequently, their development is left to chance – yet chance is a precarious foundation on which to build learning. These skills, though rarely explicitly targeted, underpin many of the broader aspirations of educational systems around the world *and* the top 10 skills identified by the WEF above.

Furthermore, a growing number of students are failing to complete their secondary schooling. In Australia, nearly 20% of enrolled students do not finish (Australian Bureau of Statistics, 2024). While there are many reasons for this, one likely contributor is students' difficulty navigating the school system. Many have never been explicitly taught how to learn, leaving them in a continual struggle to reach their academic potential and, ultimately, limiting their future employment opportunities.

Research indicates that without intentional efforts to develop self-regulation and executive functions, students are at greater risk of behavioural difficulties, underdeveloped social competencies and reduced capacity to participate as effective members of society (Rodríguez et al., 2022). This not only comes at a cost to individuals, but also to society as a whole. Economic modelling consistently shows that primary school education plays a crucial role in shaping human capital and long-term economic success. From improving cognitive skills to boosting productivity and reducing inequity, the evidence suggests that primary education is an essential investment for both individuals and national economies (Hanushek & Woessmann, 2015, 2021; Psacharopoulos & Patrinos, 2018).

Consequently, the impact of a primary school education is both significant and long-lasting. While factual and procedural knowledge are important in every area of learning, there is growing recognition that what truly matters is not just what students know, but how well they can use that knowledge. This ability to apply knowledge flexibly and meaningfully is closely tied to the development of executive functions. In a primary school setting, executive functions enable students to plan their work, manage distractions, switch between tasks and monitor their own understanding, all of which are essential when tackling unfamiliar problems or integrating new information. Without well-developed executive functions, even students with strong factual knowledge may struggle to use it effectively in complex or real-world contexts. Fostering executive function is, therefore, not separate from academic learning, but a foundational part of helping students become adaptive, independent thinkers and learners. Given this, it's no surprise that learning *how* to learn has been called the *"ultimate survival tool"* (Bjork & Bjork, 2014).

Supporting students to achieve this requires teachers to reflect on their role in setting up students to be lifelong learners (#8 on the WEF list).

This involves students taking greater ownership of their learning as they progress through the education system. A term that is gaining in popularity is *self-regulated learning* (SRL). This refers to the process by which students take control of and actively manage their own learning. It involves setting goals, monitoring progress and adjusting strategies to achieve desired outcomes. It requires students to be aware of their thinking (metacognition), emotions and behaviours as they engage with learning tasks. All these abilities are underpinned by executive functions.

I agree with the OECD (2025), which argues that "a proactive stance is necessary to enable the development of education policies and practices that are not just reactive to current challenges but are also strategically prepared for future educational demands". In line with this, intentionally developing students' executive functions is essential, as it equips them with the skills and awareness needed to understand how learning occurs and to navigate future educational challenges effectively.

In the Australian educational context, executive functions do not get much airtime. They are implicit in the General Capabilities documentation, specifically the *Personal and Social Capability*, and *Critical and Creative Thinking Capability*. They are also implicit in the IB Learner Profile (see the resources section on pages 155). Bringing them to a conscious and actionable level will help to ensure that they are actually addressed. This book is intended to do just that. Using the SOWATT framework – an acronym for Self-regulation, Organisation, Working memory, Attention, Thinking flexibly and Thinking about thinking – both teachers and students will gain an understanding of not only *why* these particular skills are critical in developing self-regulated learning, but also *how* to make this aim a reality.

A word about AI... Just a few years ago, the majority of us had no idea that AI would become such a normal part of our lives, that students would (rightly or wrongly) be using it to enhance their assignments and improve their grades, and corporations would be encouraging their workforce to interact with it as part of their role. Yet to get the best out of programs such as ChatGPT and Copilot, we still need to think critically and flexibly in order to be able to provide relevant and precise prompts. Just as important, is the ability to evaluate the accuracy of the information we are being given. Without this, we will become more vulnerable to misinformation, 'fake news' and, ultimately, more exposed to the deep and growing complexities of our technological society. I posit that well-developed self-regulatory skills can help us meet this challenge. Prioritising their development not only prepares students for life beyond school but also prevents us from falling into the trap of simply helping them cope with the present, rather than equipping them for the future.

This idea echoes the timeless wisdom of the ancient Chinese philosopher Lao Tzu, who reminds us that teaching someone a skill has far greater and lasting impact than simply providing for their immediate needs: *"Give a man a fish, and you feed him for a day; teach a man to fish, and you feed him for a lifetime."*

A helpful modern analogy is to think of teaching as helping students learn to **drive their own learning** (Hattie, 2025). Just as learner drivers need structure and support, students need guidance to develop the foundational skills – such as executive functions – that enable them to become independent learners.

When someone first learns to drive, they rely on clear rules, constant feedback and a calm instructor by their side. Gradually, they begin to take the lead, deciding when to slow down, how to handle a tricky turn or when to check the mirrors. Over time, confidence builds until they can drive independently.

Learning works the same way. If students always remain in the passenger seat, they never develop the skills to steer their own course. As educators, our role is to shift from steering for them to coaching from the passenger seat until they are ready to take the wheel, confident in their ability to learn, adapt and navigate challenges, whatever the road ahead.

A word about the layout of the book…

This book explores executive functioning in the primary school context from both the teacher's and the student's perspectives. The strategies presented in the sections towards the end of each chapter are neither finite nor prescriptive, but they *are* founded on research or drawn from solid principles from cognitive science and behavioural psychology.

They are based on 'best bets' – otherwise referred to as 'the science of learning', i.e. strategies which scientific studies have shown to be effective in supporting students to learn.

I considered grouping them into lower and upper primary strategies but concluded that, given the range of abilities within a typical primary school classroom, teachers are best placed to select the strategies suitable for their context. YOU are the best person qualified to know what is needed in your classroom with *your* students. Rather than present a long list of strategies that have the potential to be overwhelming, they have been grouped into three broad categories:

- **Mindset and Motivation** – highlighting why the skill matters and getting students invested
- **Environmental and Structural Supports** – setting up the classroom and routines to foster the skill
- **Teaching and Learning Strategies** – requiring explicit instruction and practice of the skill

What you take from each of the lists is at your discretion, however, applying strategies from each of the groups is strongly recommended to maximise your impact.

I have also included some suggestions to share with parents. In my experience, many parents are keen to support their child's learning at home but feel they lack sufficient knowledge of the 'modern curriculum' to do this adequately. I would argue that they don't need this knowledge. What we need from them is their support in helping students value learning and encourage positive study habits. This does not mean over-involvement and intervening when their child is facing mild difficulties. Students need to learn the power of persistence, productive struggle and the joy of success that comes as a result. When adults 'take over', students are more likely to have lower levels of self-regulation and independence (Leonard, 2023). The suggestions provided are not exhaustive; they are merely a prompt for you to start conversations. To use Stephen Covey's terminology, when schools and parents work together, it's a "win-win". The more consistent the expectations and actions between home and school, the greater the opportunities for students to build strong habits and set themselves up for long-term success.

Although each of the six elements of the SOWATT model is presented as a separate chapter, it is important to remember that in practice they do not operate in isolation. Executive functions are deeply interconnected, constantly overlapping and influencing one another. Their development, like learning more broadly, is neither linear nor predictable.

You will notice that some pages in this book feature a coloured icon in the top right-hand corner. These icons provide a quick reference to the relevant SOWATT element. While I encourage reading the book from cover to cover, I understand that teachers are often time-poor and may need to access information quickly. For this reason, the book is also designed so that you can dip into it and easily find guidance on specific aspects of executive functioning.

Finally, whenever I visit kindergartens using my earlier book, *Developing Executive Functioning in the Early Years: SOWATT can I do?*, some educators apologise for the state of their well-thumbed, dog-eared copies. But this always gives me joy, as it shows they are truly engaging with the content. Passive learning doesn't lead to lasting learning; to really understand, you need to get active. That is why I have intentionally left space at the end of each chapter of this book for you to summarise the key ideas and make links to what you already know, or do. As you will read in the chapter on working memory, if we don't engage with learning straight away, it is unlikely to transfer into long-term memory. This requires the brain to work a little harder and it may slow you down in the short term, but it pays off in the long run. Putting ideas into your own words deepens your understanding and helps you see how the pieces fit together.

Happy reading!

Question

What is the big idea of this book?

Chapter 1

Inside the learning brain

"The plasticity of the brain means that a student, and their teacher, have an important role in constructing it"

– International Bureau of Education, UNESCO

Learning is hard! Let's get that out in the open. If it were easy, we'd all be speaking fluent Mandarin, playing the piano like Andrea Lam and confidently using the school's photocopier without jamming it. The truth is, learning stretches the brain, tests our patience and occasionally results in tears. It's messy and it's effortful. There's also a biological reason for this. The brain is an energy-hungry organ; although it makes up only about 2% of body weight, it uses roughly 20% of the body's total energy, and in developing brains, that proportion can be even higher. When the brain is learning, it works harder, and and we feel that increased demand as effort. Harnessing brain power takes practice, persistence and energy. It's an important message to share with students.

The good news is that struggle is where the magic happens. If it weren't for those moments when a student's face lights up after finally understanding something they've been grappling with, many of us might have taken up less emotionally complex careers. We know teachers make a difference – but what if we could be even more effective by helping students take greater responsibility for their own learning, rather than seeing it as solely our job to make them learn?

An effective learner actively engages in the learning process, uses strategies to understand and remember information, and takes ownership of their progress. They don't just absorb facts, they know *how* they learn, *why* they are learning and can *apply* their knowledge in new contexts. In a primary school context, being an effective learner isn't about being the fastest or the 'best'; it's about trying hard, thinking about your learning and persisting even when things get tricky. These behaviours help develop the habits and thinking skills that support learning both now and into the future.

As children get older, the nature of learning itself changes from *primary* to *secondary* learning. Primary learning is natural, unconscious and experience-driven – children absorb information from the world around them through play, exploration and social interactions. They learn effortlessly by doing – fitting puzzle pieces together, experimenting with how far they can jump, pretending to be a firefighter. Involved adults respond to the children's interests and enrich their environment to extend their engagement and thinking.

In contrast, secondary learning is more deliberate and structured. Rather than following their own curiosity, children are taught specific content that they are expected to remember, practise and ultimately demonstrate. Activities like learning to read and write invariably require them to sit still, pay attention, follow instructions, practise repeatedly and keep going even when tasks are difficult or not inherently interesting! Success now depends not only on curiosity, but on skills such as listening, self-regulation, focus and persistence – none of which come naturally to young children.

These two forms of learning are almost polar opposites, yet we expect children to shift seamlessly from one to the other. Developing self-regulation and executive functions – mental skills like working memory, inhibitory control and cognitive flexibility – can act as a vital *bridge* between these two types of learning. Far from being optional add-ons, executive functions are the tools that make both primary and secondary learning possible and effective. To truly support children's success, they must therefore be nurtured *explicitly and intentionally*, alongside academic skills.

Part of the *learning to learn* process requires an understanding of the most complex organ in the body, one that students bring to school every day – their brain. It is an exciting time to be in education, as advances in educational neuroscience are providing answers to *why* and *how* a teaching strategy might work. It helps to take some of the guesswork out of the learning process, helping both teachers and students to become more effective in their respective roles. Sweller et al. (2011) summed it up well when they said, "Without knowledge of human cognitive processes, instructional design is blind."

The brain's plasticity is the key to learning. It is the process by which the connections between neurons are changed in response to stimulation from the environment. Although it is recognised that the brain remains plastic through life, there are periods when it is particularly responsive to change. Children's brains during the preschool to primary school age are particularly malleable. It is a period when the brain creates an abundance of neural connections and, given the correct stimulus, good habits can be formed with the least amount of effort. During adolescence the brain undergoes significant changes through a process called *neural pruning*. This refers to the process where the brain eliminates unused or less efficient connections between neurons and strengthens the ones that are more frequently used. This process helps make brain activity more efficient by refining and streamlining neural networks. The saying 'use it or lose it' is particularly relevant here; connections that are actively used and strengthened by experiences (learning, social interactions, etc.) are maintained, while those that are rarely used are discarded.

Executive functions are strongly associated with the prefrontal cortex (shown in Figure 1 overleaf), which is the slowest part of the brain to be developed, as it continues to mature well into our mid- to late 20s. It is responsible for decision-making, planning, impulse control and reasoning. While the prefrontal cortex matures, the *limbic system* (a complex network that includes the amygdala, hippocampus, parts of the prefrontal cortex as well as other structures), which controls emotions and rewards, is much more active. This imbalance means that, while young people may experience intense emotions, strong desires and heightened sensitivity to rewards, their capacity to regulate these impulses or consider long-term consequences is still under construction. As a result, they are more prone to risk-taking, impulsive decisions and being swayed by immediate gratification over thoughtful planning. Without intentional support and opportunities to strengthen executive functions, this developmental gap can lead to challenges in academic performance, relationship management and mental wellbeing, particularly during adolescence, when the push for independence is strongest, but self-regulation skills are not yet fully formed.

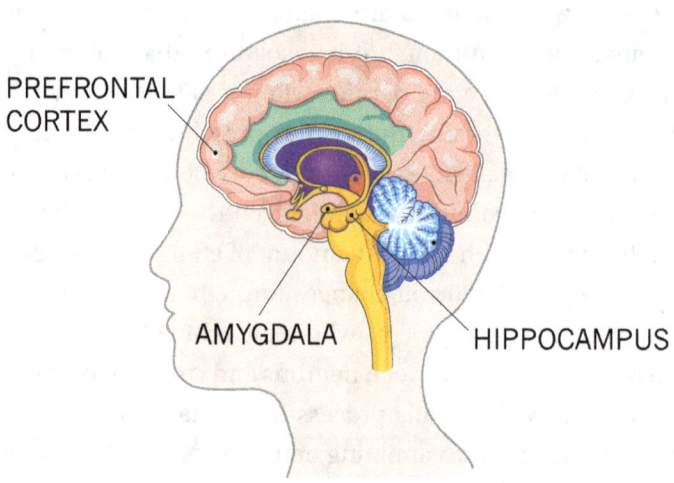

Figure 1: Key regions of the brain

A process which helps our brains become more efficient is *myelination*. It is the process of coating neurons with a fatty substance called myelin, which enables electrical signals to travel more quickly and efficiently through the brain. This process begins in early childhood and continues through adolescence, enhancing functions such as processing speed, coordination and emotional regulation. Crucially, myelination is stimulated by practice. Each time a student practises a skill, the related neural pathways are strengthened.

A helpful analogy is to imagine walking through a field of tall grass. The first time you cross it, you leave only a faint trail. If you don't walk that same path again, the grass quickly regrows and the trail disappears. But if you return to it regularly, the path becomes clearer, more defined and easier to follow. Learning works in the same way. Each time we encounter something new, a neural connection forms. Yet without reinforcement, that connection fades. With repeated practice, however, the pathway strengthens, thus increasing its efficiency.

Finally, a word about emotions. Every decision we make and every action we take is influenced by emotions. At the heart of our emotional processing is a small, almond-shaped structure deep in the brain called the *amygdala* (see Figure 1). Often referred to as the brain's emotional centre, the amygdala is involved in processing fear, anxiety and pleasure. It plays a vital role in our survival by helping us detect threats and respond appropriately. It also helps encode emotional memories, which is why emotionally charged experiences often stay with us more vividly.

The amygdala assigns emotional significance to incoming information, whether it's identifying a potential danger, like a predator, or recognising a rewarding experience. It works in close partnership with the hippocampus to store emotionally relevant memories, making those experiences easier to recall in the future. While this is essential for survival, it has implications for learning.

Under stress or fear, the amygdala can become overactive, disrupting the brain's ability to learn and retain new information. It can override the brain's rational processes, hijacking decision-making. The emotional brain takes the lead, leaving little room for calm reflection, focus or the integration of new knowledge. In essence, the amygdala acts as a gatekeeper for learning – when emotions are regulated, the gate opens; when emotions are overwhelming, the gate can slam shut. Emotion, then, can be thought of as the on/off switch of executive functioning.

In my experience, students love learning about their brains. Teaching them about their brains increases their agency. There is a plethora of engaging, age-appropriate books on the market that can be shared with students to make the process accessible. When students learn how their brains work, learning itself becomes normalised. They develop greater awareness of their own thoughts and emotions, which helps them recognise when they're feeling frustrated or stressed. With this awareness, they become more open to learning strategies that help them manage those feelings, leading to stronger emotional regulation.

Understanding that their brains are constantly changing and can grow with effort helps children develop a *growth mindset* (see page 37). They begin to see challenges as opportunities to improve, rather than obstacles that reflect their limitations. Moreover, learning about the brain's role in processing information can help children understand the importance of thinking through problems and using different strategies to find solutions. It can also help them appreciate the need to practise and repeat tasks to strengthen neural connections, which lead to automisation. When students understand that their brain sometimes reacts to stress or new situations in natural, biological ways (like fight-or-flight responses), it can reduce anxiety. They may be more likely to approach challenges calmly, knowing that their brains can adjust over time. When reluctant students understand that their brain is an active participant in learning and that the more they practise something, the more their brain strengthens, they may feel more motivated to engage in learning activities, building both confidence and interest.

From a teacher's perspective, it is important to remember that learning is a whole-brain activity. When a student is struggling, the issue may not lie with the subject matter itself, but with the underlying skills that support learning. For example, a student who finds maths challenging may actually need to strengthen their working memory, attention or impulse control to make progress.

The rapid advancements in brain science are providing us with a deeper understanding of how students process information, build connections and retain knowledge. With this knowledge, we are able to create more effective, evidence-based teaching strategies that align with the brain's natural learning preferences. This is a golden opportunity to refine our practice: support and foster the conditions that increase the likelihood of students who can *thrive*, rather than just survive, and start to *drive* their own learning.

My summary

What are your key takeaways?

How does this chapter relate to what you already know or do?

Chapter 2

Introducing the SOWATT approach

"If you are not willing to learn, no one can help you. If you are determined to learn, no one can stop you"

– Zig Ziglar

Before launching into the SOWATT approach, it's time to define what executive functions are.

In essence, they are the cognitive skills that enable us to juggle our busy lives. They are the mental processes that enable students to focus attention, manage time, follow instructions, hold and manipulate information, and adapt to new or unexpected situations. When we intentionally teach and model these skills, we equip students with tools to plan, stay organised, regulate their emotions and persist through challenges. By embedding executive function support into everyday classroom practice, we're not only helping students succeed academically, but also fostering the foundational skills they need to become lifelong, independent learners.

To get a better sense of how executive functions help us throughout the day, meet Ryan, a Year 5 student who struggles with his executive functioning.

Time	Behaviour	Executive function difficulty
8am	Ryan knows he has library class today, but he can't find his book. He goes back to his bedroom and eventually finds it under the pile of clothes on the floor. He walks past the checklist his mum made with him the night before and runs to join his dad in the car feeling very agitated.	- Emotional regulation - Organisation - Attention - Working memory
11am	Ryan's teacher asks the class how last night's reading relates to the words on the whiteboard. Ryan has no idea. He is mentally thinking about all the steps it will take to answer the question. He's feeling overwhelmed.	- Working memory - Emotional regulation
1pm	Lunchtime! Ryan sits at a table with his friends. He sees that Liam has a heap of salami in his lunchbox, so he reaches over and takes a slice. He then sees his friend Tony and calls out to him to join the group. He is unaware that the teacher on duty is glaring at him and on the verge of reprimanding him.	- Impulse control - Self-monitoring - Attention
4pm	At an after-school soccer game, Ryan joins his friends. His best friend is put in the other team, but Ryan keeps forgetting and passes him the ball when his friend calls his name. His teammates get angry with him for letting the team down, although Ryan is oblivious to the fact.	- Impulse control - Working memory - Cognitive flexibly - Metacognition
6pm	Back home, it's Ryan's job to lay the table. He forgets to put out the water glasses and his little sister makes fun of him. It soon erupts into a screaming match.	- Organisation - Working memory - Emotional regulation
7:15pm	Ryan sits down to do his maths homework only to find he has left it at school. He could make a start on the research for his project on Ecosystems instead, but he can't shift his thinking. He's too worried about what his teacher will say tomorrow about not doing his maths.	- Organisation - Cognitive flexibility - Emotional regulation
8pm	Time to call it a day, Ryan goes into the bathroom to get ready for bed. He's still thinking about his maths homework and doesn't look where he's going – bang! He walks straight into the corner of the cabinet. It hurts! Ryan brushes his teeth as fast as he can and jumps into bed, his heart racing and his shin stinging.	- Cognitive flexibility - Attention - Emotional regulation

There's good news for students like Ryan; growing evidence shows that, unless limited by serious health conditions, all children have the capacity to learn effectively and possess significant intrinsic potential (Shonkoff & Phillips, 2000). While some may need more support than others, all benefit from teachers who are skilled in helping them develop their executive functions.

For teachers, there is a further need to understand executive functioning due to increasing numbers of neurodiverse students in our classrooms. Many have diagnoses linked to underdeveloped executive function skills, such as attention deficit hyperactivity disorder (ADHD) and autism spectrum disorder (ASD). Every day, classroom teachers encounter behaviours that can challenge even the most experienced. Traditionally, our response has been reactive, addressing these behaviours as they arise. But what if we could flip this approach on its head? I agree with Martin Seligman, who advocates that, it's time to move away from the "disease model" and adopt a more proactive, strengths-based framework. Imagine if we were able to offer *all* students the best possible conditions for executive functions to thrive, and have strategies we could intentionally use to enhance them further? The chances are, we would not only be able to identify difficulties in their early stages, but put better support in place, increasing the odds for *all* students to become successful learners.

To that end, every teacher needs a strong understanding of the role executive functions play in learning and wellbeing. With this knowledge, we are better equipped to foster these skills and support students in becoming successful, independent learners. A substantial body of research shows that executive function interventions have a positive impact on student outcomes, particularly for those from low-income backgrounds. Emerging evidence suggests that such interventions can help close gaps in inequities rooted in early disadvantage, enabling students to unlock their learning potential (Blair & Raver, 2015).

Anecdotally, based on my own experience, I would posit that students from more affluent backgrounds are also in need of these skills. Too often, well-meaning parents (think helicopter or lawnmower parents) can overindulge their offspring, shielding them from the challenges, frustration and natural consequences of their actions. While the intent is to protect and support, this overinvolvement can inadvertently limit opportunities for children to develop resilience, self-control, problem-solving skills and independence – all of which are core components of good executive functioning. Without the chance to practise navigating setbacks, managing their own time or making and learning from mistakes, these students may enter adulthood academically capable, but ill-equipped to handle the complexities of life beyond school. This underscores the universality of executive function development as an essential goal for all learners, regardless of socioeconomic background.

I draw on the work of Shonkoff and Phillips (2000) and McCoy and Sabol (2025), defining self-regulation and executive function as:

> *"A broad set of cognitive skills that are used to purposefully monitor and manage our thoughts, emotions and actions in the service of reaching a particular goal."*

The SOWATT approach to developing self-regulation and executive functions

Three skills are frequently highlighted as being the core executive functions: inhibitory control (the ability to stop or suppress predominant responses), working memory (holding and manipulating information in the mind) and cognitive or mental flexibility (the ability to shift attention and to think in different ways). Many researchers – myself included – would argue that executive function is broader than this. Acknowledging the ongoing debate regarding exactly which skills fall under the executive function umbrella, in the SOWATT framework the focus is on:

- **S**elf-regulation
- **O**rganisation
- **W**orking memory
- **A**ttention
- **T**hinking flexibly
- **T**hinking about thinking

Mastering these six skills enables students to innovate, manage competing information, and thrive in environments marked by diversity and change. While each skill is generally considered distinct, they are deeply interconnected. For example, using inhibitory control requires working memory to hold the appropriate (rather than an impulsive) response in mind. But to retain that response, the student first needs to have focused their attention on the relevant information.

The SOWATT approach is underpinned by seven evidence-based principles:

1. **Biology is not our destiny** – our genes might be the blueprint, but our environment and experiences affect *how* the brain develops (Jacob & Parkinson, 2015).
2. **Start early** – the preschool years are a time of rapid brain development, but this growth does not stop once children enter primary school. In the early primary years, it is especially important that strong neural pathways continue to be reinforced and extended, as this is when children are building the foundations for more complex learning (Diamond & Ling, 2016).
3. **Repetition** – ongoing daily practice produces greater improvements than lessons only once or twice per week (Diamond & Lee, 2011).
4. **Challenge** – executive functions must be continually challenged at an appropriate level to see improvements – ideally at the Zone of Proximal Development (ZPD) (Diamond, 2016).
5. **Engagement** – executive function activities should be age appropriate and build self-confidence and agency (Raver et al., 2011).
6. **Transfer** – global training of executive functions = greater transfer effects (McClelland et al., 2019).
7. **Teacher knowledge** – this is more important than expensive equipment (Madanipour et al., 2025).

Based on personal experience, I would add an eighth one to the list: *Intentionality*. As teachers, you may accept and agree with all seven of the above principles, but unless you intentionally make the effort to plan for and implement some of the practices suggested in this book, monitor and evaluate their impact, it is unlikely that your students' executive functioning will be enhanced to their full potential. Instead, their development will be left to chance, and students will be unlikely to be able to drive their learning.

Historically, two broad perspectives have shaped our understanding of executive functions. One treats them as a **unitary construct**, emphasising their interconnectedness and suggesting they cannot be meaningfully studied in isolation. The other takes a **componential view**, considering each executive function as a distinct ability. While evidence exists for both perspectives, the literature increasingly points towards an **integrated approach**, especially in the early years of schooling. What is clear is that executive functions do not develop in isolation – growth in one area often produces gains in another, ultimately strengthening the system as a whole.

Adopting a broader approach and fostering executive function development across contexts and curriculum subjects increases the opportunities for transfer. However, a caveat to this is the recognition that although individual tasks draw on more than one ability concurrently, there will be tasks – for example, mental arithmetic – that will draw more heavily on one executive function than another. In the example of mental arithmetic, working memory is absolutely vital in allowing the numbers to be manipulated mentally.

Influences on the development of executive functions

Now that we have established what executive functions are, it is important to consider the key factors that shape their development. The SOWATT model highlights four central influences, shown in Figure 2: a student's genetic makeup, their environment, the experiences they encounter and the role of their teacher.

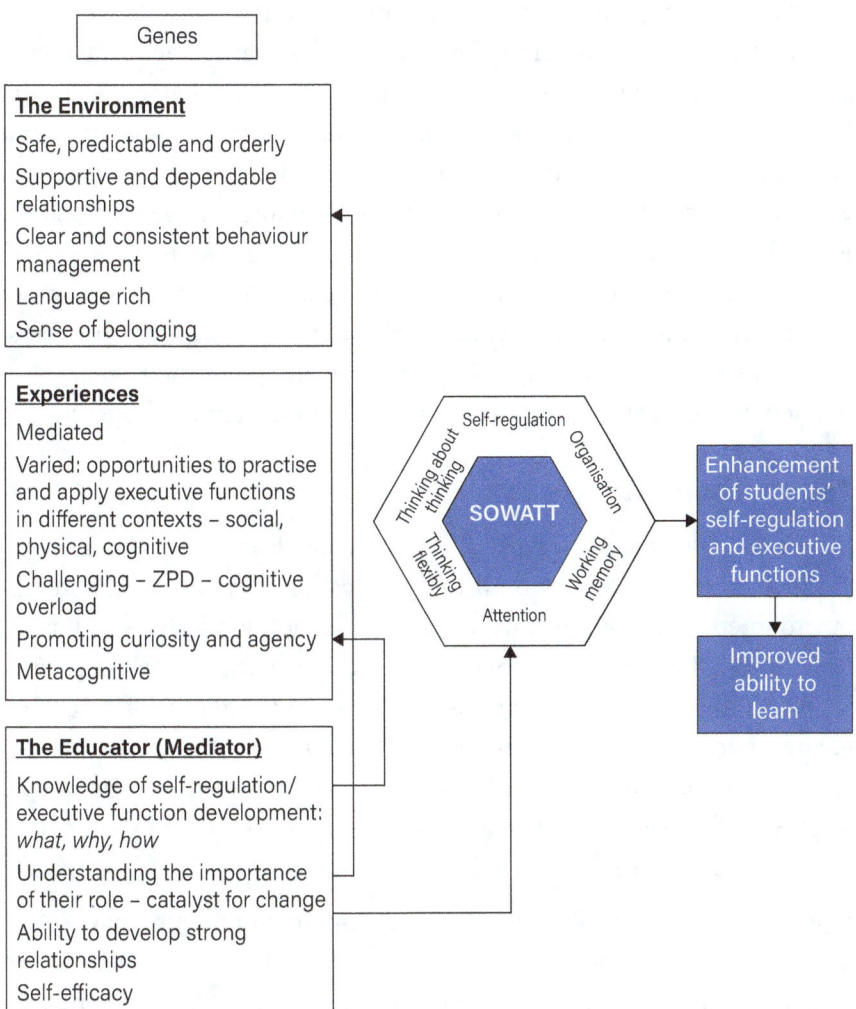

Figure 2: The SOWATT model

Genes

Each of us is born into circumstances over which we have no control. Genes, economic resources, education, health status and environments are passed on to us through our families and neighbourhoods. These factors play a significant role in shaping the trajectories of our lives. This is all well and good if you happen to win the lottery of birth, but for those who don't, whose lives are impacted by trauma, poverty and insecure relationships, there needs to be some hope. A potentially equalising factor is access to high-quality education. Numerous studies have documented that cognitive ability predicts schooling, wages, participation in crime and success in many facets of life (Heckman, 2011; Spengler et al., 2018). Character traits such as perseverance, motivation, self-esteem and self-control work alongside cognition and can change future social and economic status (Heckman, 2011). There is, therefore, a need for teachers to understand the factors that affect the development of executive functions, as they underpin both cognitive and character aspirations. In so doing, teachers are well placed to set their classrooms up as environments where executive functions are likely to thrive and tailor their practice to provide the best possible opportunities to promote their development.

The environment

In school, teachers are responsible for their classroom environment. The environment refers to both the physical and emotional classroom environment. We need to consider not just what it looks like, but how it feels. After all, we all remember how a teacher made us feel long after we remember what they taught us. Ultimately, we are striving to create environments in which the brain can function at its best. To echo the words of Hendrick and MacPherson (2017), "there is an ethical imperative to provide the best possible classroom conditions in which students in our charge can flourish".

Safe, predictable and orderly classroom environments may seem obvious; however, it is important to explain why this is vital. Depending on where you work, you are likely to have children from a range of different backgrounds in your class – or at the very least, from families with different approaches to parenting. The classroom needs to be somewhere where students feel safe and have a sense of belonging, in order to thrive, regardless of their family circumstances. This is achieved in a number of ways; two significant ways are: i) routines, and ii) good classroom management.

Routines help students feel safe, as by their very nature, routines are predictable. They are as crucial for the shy, nervous student, as for the student who breezes into the classroom full of energy and raring to go. The former will be comforted by knowing there is a rhythm to the day, and the latter needs routines to keep their energy in check – two different causes of emotional regulation which clear morning routines can help to address. Our brains like predictability, they naturally look for patterns (du Castel, 2015). Doing certain things in a particular order at roughly the same time every day helps strengthen brain connections and builds self-confidence because students know what to expect. Routines also require the brain to use less energy, which can then be used for learning new things.

The physical layout of the classroom needs to be considered. Classrooms are spaces for learning, so design them to support that purpose. Consider and address any factors that might interfere with students' ability to focus. Think about the seating arrangement – how does it support students' ability to see and hear instruction? What is on the walls? How does it support or distract students from learning? For example, pinboards dedicated to students' birthdays might be better situated at the back rather than the front of the class!

Students need to be able to expect and find **supportive and dependable relationships** in the classroom. In an unpredictable world, the importance of healthy, trusting relationships cannot be overstated, especially for students who may not experience them consistently at home. For some children, your classroom may be the only place where they feel truly seen, valued and safe. And it's much easier to learn when someone recognises your worth.

Take the time to get to know your students as individuals; know their 'currency' or what makes them tick: their family background, interests, hobbies, even their favourite footy team. This knowledge becomes incredibly powerful when students are dysregulated. It allows you to engage, distract, comfort or persuade in ways that are meaningful to them, helping to de-escalate emotional moments. Strong teacher-student relationships are the foundation for emotional safety in the classroom. They reduce anxiety, increase engagement and curiosity, and encourage persistence when learning gets tough. Connection truly is the gateway to cognition.

It should be clear by now that the classroom needs to be a relatively stress-free environment. Stress is the enemy of thinking. The reason we struggle to think clearly under stress is linked to the amygdala, the brain's emotional control centre. This process is the same for children as it is for adults. That's why it's so important that we manage our own emotions before we attempt to coregulate others. Creating an inclusive and responsive classroom environment means being attuned to the emotional states of all learners, recognising when stress may be interfering with their ability to engage, and responding with empathy and support. When students feel emotionally safe and valued, they are far more able to think, reflect and learn effectively.

A growing body of evidence highlights the importance of **language-rich** environments. Language scaffolds thinking. Therefore, if a student's oral language is underdeveloped, they are unlikely to be able to express their feelings and emotions verbally. Instead, they resort to non-verbal language, which in highly charged emotional situations invariably includes behaviours such as hitting, kicking and screaming. One of the core features of emotional development includes the ability to identify and understand one's own feelings. There is a need, therefore, to teach the language to describe emotions so that students can express themselves in words rather than physical actions. As Professor Marc Brackett (2019) says, "You need to be able to name it to tame it."

Language, and vocabulary development in particular, has been shown to be related to a child's family background. Students from lower socioeconomic backgrounds tend to enter primary school knowing fewer words than their peers from more affluent families. This gap usually remains throughout primary education, unless addressed, since understanding and using a range of vocabulary supports the early stages of reading development and is crucial for reading comprehension. It cannot be assumed, therefore, that students – especially the younger ones, have the words to describe how they are feeling. No wonder their actions are louder than words!

The language used by adults plays a crucial role in shaping the development of executive functions (Madanipour et al., 2025). As teachers, it is important to reflect on how we interact with students and consider ways to enhance these interactions. One approach gaining traction in education is *Responsive Teaching*, which aligns well with fostering executive functioning and the concept of *learning to learn*. This approach emphasises explicit instruction, making the teacher's expectations clear and reducing ambiguity. For many students, this clarity can lower stress levels and decrease cognitive load (see page 73). Responsive teaching also prioritises engaging students in deeper thinking through open-ended questions that require them to justify their reasoning. Additionally, it involves providing positive, targeted feedback in real time, helping students build self-awareness about their learning process and identify concrete steps to improve (Darling-Hammond, 2000; Hattie & Timperley, 2007). These approaches will be unpacked further in Chapter 8, which discusses the importance of language in relation to metacognition, or thinking about thinking.

In the SOWATT model, language may be viewed as 'the conceptual glue' that brings all the different parts together. Language allows executive functions to be targeted and practised in different situations and contexts throughout the day rather than at isolated times. In a typical day, students interact with teachers and peers across a variety of, each providing different, yet equally important, opportunities for instruction, interaction and the active use of executive functions. Recognising language as one of the important mechanisms for change further highlights the recognition that learning, particularly in primary school students, is a socially embedded and active process.

Experiences

Earlier, I emphasised the importance of reducing stress in the classroom. This should not be mistaken for removing challenge; on the contrary, without consistent and appropriate challenges to our executive functions, they are unlikely to develop fully. This is significant when we start examining the experiences that are presented to students.

Vygotsky's Zone of Proximal Development (1978) (the 'sweet spot') describes tasks that sit just beyond a learner's current unaided ability but are achievable with the right support. In this zone, students must do effortful thinking, sometimes referred to as 'productive struggle'. It is this 'struggle' that strengthens thinking skills. If the task is too easy, students switch off from effort and learning stalls; if it's too hard, they get frustrated, anxious or give up. Both extremes reduce engagement and raise the chance of dysregulated behaviour.

For example, if a Year 4 class is given a multistep word problem that asks them to plan a shopping list on a limited budget…

- **In the 'sweet spot':** The problem requires reading carefully, holding several numbers in mind, choosing which items to buy, checking totals and adjusting when the budget is exceeded. With a small amount of teacher scaffolding (a graphic organiser showing steps, a worked example or a prompt question like 'What's your first step?'), most students feel challenged but capable. They practise planning, holding and manipulating information, resisting an impulsive first choice and reflecting on their strategies.
- **Too easy:** If every child is given a one-line arithmetic question, students who already know the skill become bored, fidget, talk or daydream. Boredom reduces sustained attention and willingness to use effortful strategies – the same executive processes that would be strengthened by appropriately difficult tasks.
- **Too hard:** If the teacher gives a multistep budgeting task with unfamiliar vocabulary and no scaffolds, many students will feel overwhelmed. Anxiety narrows attention, working memory gets overloaded, impulsive responses increase ("I'll just pick the first things") and some students may shut down, refuse to engage or act out.

Planning for cognitive challenge is, therefore, important and needs to be considered before starting an activity. It is not enough to simply provide an experience to practise a skill, we should be aiming for the 'sweet spot'. Incremental increases in challenge need to be planned in response to what we are seeing in our students' learning. This can be achieved either by raising or lowering the level of cognition, or by increasing or decreasing the complexity of the task. *Task analysis* prior in the planning phase and flexible *scaffolding* in the process phase of learning is, therefore, vital.

Conducting **task analyses** requires teachers to anticipate cognitive challenges and plan more effectively for student success. Young learners are still developing their executive functioning skills, and a task that seems simple to an adult may involve multiple steps and skills for a child. By analysing a task, teachers can identify each step, and the skills required to achieve it. This makes it easier to pinpoint where students might struggle or conversely need to be extended. With a clear breakdown of a task, instruction is more focused, efficient and will be more responsive to students' needs.

Scaffolding involves providing temporary support to help students in their learning. The aim is to help students achieve independence in their learning by gradually reducing support as they become more competent. Scaffolding bridges the gap between what students can do on their own and what they can do with guidance. It helps students move from novice to independent learners. As teachers, a real concern we have is, *"Where is the line between helping the student and 'enabling' the student?"* To help us address this question, a useful model, which has been around for a very long time but is worth revisiting, is the *Gradual Release of Responsibility Model* developed by Pearson and Gallagher back in 1983. Essentially, the four stages shown below guide a teacher's practice:

1. **Focused Instruction (I do)**
    - The teacher models the skill, concept or strategy explicitly.
    - Students observe, listen and take in the information.

2. **Guided Instruction (We do it together)**
    - The teacher provides guided practice with students.
    - Students begin participating with teacher support.

3. **Collaborative Learning (You work together)**
    - Students work in pairs or small groups to practise the skill.
    - The teacher provides minimal but necessary guidance.

4. **Independent Learning (You do it by yourself)**
    - Students apply their knowledge independently.
    - The teacher observes and assesses student understanding.

Scaffolding can take several different forms, including templates to support writing, verbal cues or simply reminders written in a student's diary. Implicit in this scaffolding process is the idea that teachers will be continually checking for understanding and adapting their teaching strategies based on ongoing feedback.

Language is a vital tool in scaffolding. Teachers need to adjust the level of language support based on the student's current abilities. This may be as simple as a teacher modelling how to solve a maths problem by thinking out loud, demonstrating the process step by step and reducing this support as students become more comfortable with the process. As students become more capable, the language used to describe tasks can become more complex. It acts as both a bridge and a barrier; directly influencing how students access, process and engage with learning. The way language is used by the teacher, peers or within instructional materials can either lighten the cognitive load (see page 73) or raise it by encouraging deeper thinking and more precise communication.

Introducing and intentionally using subject-specific vocabulary is one powerful way to increase cognitive challenge. For example, in a Year 5 science lesson on chemical changes, prompting students to describe what they observe using terms like *reactants, products, irreversible change* and *temperature-dependent reaction* invites them to go beyond surface-level observations and begin thinking like scientists.

In literacy, instead of asking students to *"Write a story"*, asking them to *"Compose a narrative that includes a complication, resolution and character development"* raises the task's complexity while embedding key curriculum concepts. Similarly, in maths, shifting from *"What is the answer to this problem?"* to *"Can you explain your reasoning using the terms 'estimate', 'strategy' and 'justify'?"* fosters metacognitive reflection and encourages mathematical discussion.

By carefully considering the language we use – whether simplifying or enriching instructions, questions or feedback – we can influence how deeply students engage with the material. Clear, challenging and thought-provoking language promotes higher-order thinking and deeper learning, while overly simplistic or directive language can reduce cognitive engagement.

The importance of the teacher

Teachers play a pivotal role in developing students' executive functions. They are uniquely placed not only to teach learning strategies explicitly, but also to create classroom environments that encourage students to take ownership of their learning and apply these strategies independently.

Figure 3: Teachers' role in developing students' executive functions

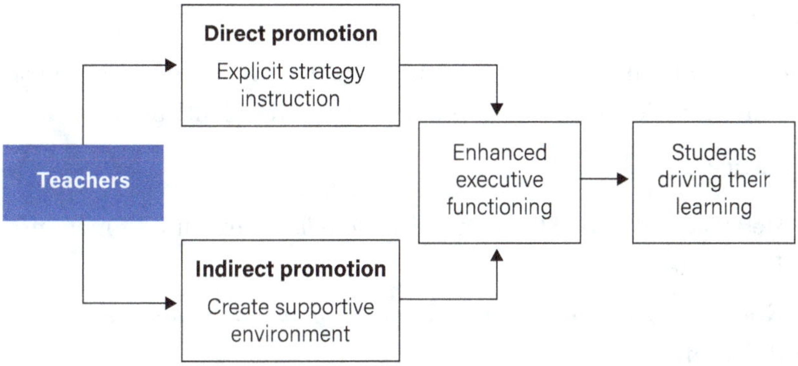

```
                    ┌─────────────────────┐
                    │  Direct promotion   │
              ┌────▶│ Explicit strategy   │────┐
              │     │    instruction      │    │
              │     └─────────────────────┘    ▼
      ┌───────────┐                      ┌──────────┐      ┌──────────┐
      │ Teachers  │                      │ Enhanced │      │ Students │
      │           │                      │ executive│─────▶│ driving  │
      │           │                      │functioning│     │ their    │
      └───────────┘                      └──────────┘      │ learning │
              │     ┌─────────────────────┐    ▲           └──────────┘
              │     │ Indirect promotion  │    │
              └────▶│ Create supportive   │────┘
                    │    environment      │
                    └─────────────────────┘
```

Since executive functions are not fixed traits, they develop through repeated practice in meaningful contexts. Teachers create those contexts every day. They:

- Model self-regulation in how they manage the classroom, solve problems and respond to challenges.
- Structure environments that allow children to practise planning, organising, shifting attention and persisting with tasks.
- Design learning experiences that extend thinking.
- Provide feedback and scaffolding so that students can gradually take more responsibility for their own thinking and behaviour.

In addition, teachers bring with them their beliefs, values, knowledge, experience and motivation, which profoundly shape their capacity to foster executive functions in students.

Beliefs: These include teachers' convictions about how children learn, the malleability of the brain and the importance of self-regulation.

Values: Teachers who value self-directed learning might create classrooms that encourage planning, problem solving and reflection.

Knowledge: Knowledgeable teachers can explicitly teach executive functioning strategies, scaffold tasks appropriately and adjust expectations to developmental levels.

Experience: Experienced teachers can recognise when students struggle with executive functions, and can identify triggers and provide timely support.

Motivation: Highly motivated teachers are more likely to persist in using executive function-promoting routines, even when challenging.

In essence...

- **Beliefs & Values** → Shape the *why* and *what* of executive function-focused teaching
- **Knowledge & Experience** → Shape the *how* (strategies, scaffolding, differentiation)
- **Motivation** → Drives consistency and creativity in applying strategies

From a sustainability perspective, teachers are our best chance of making long-term differences. Essentially, they act as 'sustainability catalysts' for human potential. By embedding executive function development into everyday teaching, the impact reaches every child, not just those in targeted programs, making it an equitable and scalable approach. The executive function skills they foster don't fade; they compound over a lifetime.

Context plays a crucial role in shaping educational practices, and it's essential to recognise that 'one size does not fit all'. This is why the SOWATT framework presented in this book is not intended as an add-on to an already packed curriculum. Instead, it serves as a lens through which we can examine and adapt teacher and student practices to fit the unique needs of each context. When considering students within their specific context, it's important to remember that both student and adult behaviours are shaped by the social environment in which they operate. These behaviours are also influenced by the broader cultural norms that surround them. Expectations for executive functions and self-regulation, for example, will vary significantly across different educational stages, whether in kindergarten, primary school or university, because they are inherently shaped by the societal context in which they occur.

SOWATT do students bring to the table?

Mindset

Many will be familiar with Carol Dweck's work on mindsets (2015), and I encourage you to refer to her work for a more detailed understanding. In brief, *mindset* refers to the underlying beliefs and attitudes a person holds about their abilities, potential and the world around them. It can significantly shape how one approaches challenges, learning and growth. Students with a growth mindset believe that abilities can be developed through effort and using effective strategies. They are more likely to persist when tasks feel hard, use feedback to improve and see mistakes as a part of learning. This mindset activates and sustains the very executive functions they need: it supports inhibitory control (resisting the urge to give up), working memory (holding strategies in mind) and cognitive flexibility (trying a different approach when stuck). Conversely, a fixed mindset can make students more likely to give up when faced with difficulty. Believing that their abilities are fixed and that struggle is a sign of not being 'smart enough', they may disengage quickly when a task feels challenging. This means they miss valuable opportunities to practise and strengthen their executive functions.

It's really important that learning in school helps students see mistakes as a normal and useful part of the process, not something to avoid, but something to learn from. They need to know that getting things wrong is actually how we figure out how to get things right. We also want students to start taking more responsibility for their own thinking and learning, so they're not always relying on the teacher or support staff to help them make necessary shifts in their thinking. After all, we're not just preparing them to pass tests, we're helping them build skills they'll use for life.

To help students develop confidence as capable and successful learners, teachers also need to be aware of their own mindset and the attitudes they are subconsciously projecting. Two specific factors that need to be addressed are:

1. The teacher's own beliefs about intelligence and the learning process. This is especially true in maths instruction. There's a pervasive myth of the 'maths person', in which only certain people

can master the subject, and research suggests it's important to tackle this myth head-on.

2. The manner in which the teacher provides feedback to students. This is particularly important for students who struggle, who can construe criticism of their work as a sign that a teacher is biased or doubts their intelligence. To combat this outcome, teachers are encouraged to provide 'WISE' feedback that conveys high standards and assures students that they can meet them. It can be particularly useful for students who may feel uncertain or disengaged.

WISE feedback draws on research from motivation and equity in education, including studies by researchers like Geoffrey Cohen, Claude Steele and Lee Ross (1999). WISE is an acronym for:

- **W**arm: The feedback begins with a positive, respectful tone that shows the teacher cares about the student's effort and growth.
- **I**nsightful: The feedback offers clear insight into how the student can improve, often framed as part of a learning journey.
- **S**pecific: The advice is concrete and actionable, not vague. It focuses on *what* needs to be improved and *how* to do it.
- **E**ncouraging: It conveys belief in the student's ability to succeed, often reinforcing that the teacher has high expectations *because* they believe in the student's potential.

In practice, it might sound like:

> "You've made a strong start with your introduction – well done. To strengthen your argument, try adding one more example to support your point. I know you're capable of this, and I'm excited to see your next draft."

Confidence and self-efficacy

Confidence, executive functions and emotions are deeply interconnected in learning. When students feel confident, they are more likely to *use* their executive function skills effectively, which in turn helps them regulate their emotions and persist with challenging tasks. A confident learner believes in their general capabilities and, as a result, is more willing to take risks, try something challenging and keep going when things don't work the first time. Confidence is strengthened through successful use of executive functions – when a student plans, completes and reflects on a task, this experience of success builds their overall belief in themselves and increases their motivation to engage again.

Self-efficacy, while related, is more task-specific and more easily influenced by success, feedback and learning experiences. When students *believe* they can plan a project, resist distractions or switch strategies, they are more likely to *activate* the executive functions linked to those behaviours. Research shows that high self-efficacy supports goal setting (linked to organisation), task initiation and persistence (linked to working memory and inhibition), and self-monitoring and reflection (metacognition). Unsurprisingly, learners with high self-efficacy tend to achieve better academic outcomes – not simply because they are more able, but because they *believe their efforts matter* and therefore apply themselves more strategically.

Understanding how the brain works can help students strengthen both their confidence and self-efficacy. One powerful idea to share with them is the role of the *Reticular Activating System* (RAS): the brain's internal 'filter'. Every second, the brain receives far more information than it can consciously process, so the RAS decides what to pay attention to based on what seems most important in that moment. This is helpful until negative thinking takes over. The RAS is like a mini Google: it scans for evidence to support whatever you're thinking or asking. So, if a child repeatedly asks, *"Why am I so bad at this?"*, the RAS will start searching for examples to prove that thought correct, reinforcing a negative mindset and weakening both confidence and self-belief.

The key, then, is to teach students to ask themselves *better* questions; questions that turn their RAS towards solutions, strengths and possibilities instead of problems. With practice, this more constructive thinking builds stronger confidence, enhances self-efficacy and creates the emotional climate that allows executive functions to flourish.

Motivation

Motivation is the difference between intention and action (Ryan & Deci, 2000). It is key in the self-regulated learning approach, fostering both engagement and positive behaviours. Motivation helps students set meaningful goals. When students are motivated, they are more likely to identify specific learning objectives, plan how to achieve them and use strategies like time management or breaking tasks into smaller steps. Without motivation, students may struggle to form or commit to goals, leading to a lack of direction.

Motivated students are also more likely to initiate tasks promptly and maintain focus on them for longer periods. If motivation is low, students may procrastinate or become distracted more easily, impacting their ability to engage with the material fully. A lack of motivation can lead to frustration, disengagement or giving up on tasks that seem difficult (Schunk et al., 2014).

It is important to remember that motivation is heavily influenced by success. The feeling you get when you are successful at something is due to the release of a chemical in the brain called dopamine. When dopamine is released, it actually increases students' capacities to control attention and store long-term memories. Therefore, if you want students to be motivated, it is vital that they experience success, because when you get better at something, you feel good about yourself and are more likely to invest time doing more of that activity. This was clearly illustrated in the 2016 study by Garon-Carrier et al., who found that prior mathematics achievement seemed to influence a student's subsequent intrinsic motivation to learn maths, rather than the other way around. As teachers, we need to bear in mind how we ensure that this happens, because we all know instances where repeated failures can lead to negative emotions that lead to a lack of motivation, which in turn disrupt executive functions, thus, creating a vicious cycle which makes it difficult to engage executive functions and is also difficult to break.

Sense of agency and autonomy

Agency is central to developing executive functioning and ultimately self-regulated learning because it empowers students to take ownership of their thinking, behaviour and learning strategies. It helps students build their capacity to *set goals*, *plan* and *monitor progress*. When students feel they have a say in what and how they learn, they're more likely to persist through challenges and manage their time and attention effectively. Self-regulated learners are motivated from within. Agency builds intrinsic motivation by giving students meaningful choices and a sense of purpose. When students experience success through their own effort and decision-making, it reinforces metacognitive awareness and self-efficacy. Developing agency isn't about giving students free rein, it's about structured autonomy, where students are *guided* to make choices, *taught* to think strategically and *supported* to take increasing responsibility for their learning. Ways to intentionally develop it include fostering a classroom culture of student voice and reflection and adopting student-led conferences alongside teacher/parent evenings.

Unpacking the SOWATT elements

Figure 4 overleaf provides an overview of what to expect in each of the SOWATT elements. As mentioned previously, development is dynamic, uneven and highly individual, which is why supporting these skills requires patience, flexibility and a long-term perspective. At times, one skill may appear stronger, while another lags behind, only to shift again as students encounter new experiences, challenges and contexts.

Figure 4: The SOWATT framework

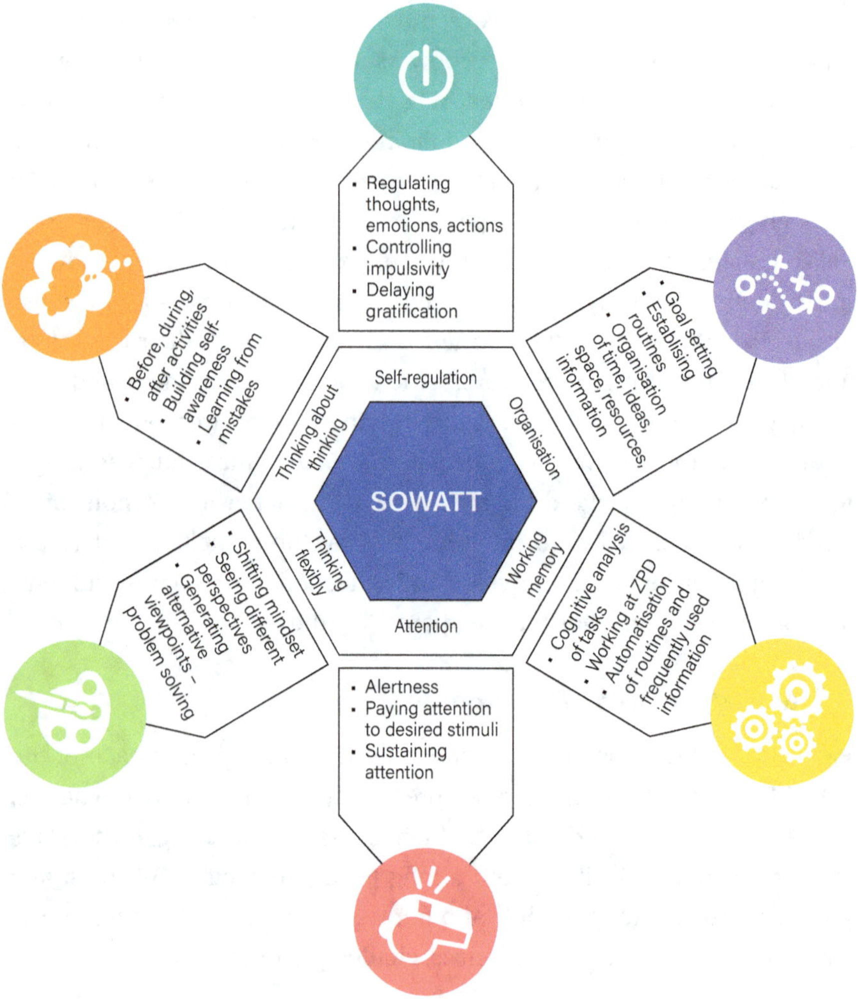

- Regulating thoughts, emotions, actions
- Controlling impulsivity
- Delaying gratification

Self-regulation

- Goal setting
- Establishing routines
- Organisation of time, ideas, space, resources, information

Organisation

- Before, during, after activities
- Building self-awareness
- Learning from mistakes

Thinking about thinking

SOWATT

- Cognitive analysis of tasks
- Working at ZPD
- Automatisation of routines and frequently used information

Working memory

- Shifting mindset
- Seeing different perspectives
- Generating alternative viewpoints – problem solving

Thinking flexibly

- Alertness
- Paying attention to desired stimuli
- Sustaining attention

Attention

42 Developing Executive Functioning in the Primary Years

My summary

What are your key takeaways?

How does this chapter relate to what you already know or do?

Chapter 3

Self-regulation

"Until we teach our kids to self-regulate, we will be stuck trying to reason with their unreasonable brain, which will only leave everyone stuck in the cycle of conflict"

– Bill Crawford

The link between self-regulation and executive functions, and the need to develop them simultaneously

'Self-regulation' is a phrase that gets used frequently in schools, usually in association with students' behaviour. Self-control, self-discipline, self-management, composure, restraint, willpower and discipline are also words that may spring to mind when considering the term. This plethora of terminology has led to a jingle-jangle fallacy, whereby the same term is defined differently, and different terms are used to describe the same phenomena. Although there are numerous definitions of self-regulation (see Burman et al., 2015), one conceptualisation that has come to the fore is:

> *"Self-regulation is the ability to control our attention and thinking, behaviours, emotional reactions, and social interactions, despite any impulses or distractions to the contrary"* (Howard & Vasseleu, 2020).

Reading this, it becomes clear that self-regulation is multifaceted – it is more than just good behaviour. Essentially, it has two sides: first, it involves the capacity to control impulses and to *stop* doing something, if needed, and second, it relies on the capacity to *do* something – even if you don't want to do it. Self-regulated students can delay gratification and suppress their immediate impulses enough to think ahead to the possible consequences of their actions, or consider alternative actions that would be more appropriate – in both instances this is achieved by the student using their executive functions.

Self-regulation is widely recognised as a foundational skill for success. Together with executive functioning, it is one of the strongest predictors of school readiness, academic achievement and lifelong wellbeing. Rightly or wrongly, school systems are largely built around students' ability to self-regulate (see the two types of learning on page 14). This can be seen in the Year 1 child expected to sit quietly on the mat while listening to instructions, as well as the high school student expected to focus on a document on the screen rather than give in to the temptation of checking social media.

Students with good self-regulation skills can focus on tasks longer, follow instructions and persist in the face of challenges, leading to better academic outcomes. But it is not just useful for learning; self-regulated students are better at managing conflicts, cooperating with peers and navigating social situations, fostering positive relationships (Blair & Raver, 2015). When students can regulate their emotions, they are less likely to experience extreme stress or anxiety and are better equipped to cope with frustration or disappointment.

Conversely, students with poor self-regulation will often get themselves into trouble through impulsive behaviour. Studies have found an association between a student's poor self-regulation and a negative relationship with their educator (Xu, et al., 2024). In the longer term, poor self-regulation in primary school students has been linked to an increased risk of developing later behaviour problems, greater risk-taking behaviour in adolescence and disordered behaviour as adults. Therefore, being able to self-regulate benefits not only students, but society as a whole.

Interestingly, a 2018 study by Edossa and colleagues found that behaviour regulation at age 7 had a substantial and positive effect on teachers' evaluations of educational achievement during the final year of primary school at the age of 11. Teachers' perceptions are invariably transmitted to the student, either intentionally or otherwise. It should not be a surprise, therefore, to learn that students lacking in self-regulation invariably have a poor relationship with teachers (Raver, 2002) and are, therefore, more likely to lose motivation to engage in the learning process and even disengage with the schooling system.

An increasing number of researchers – myself included – highlight the considerable overlap between executive functions and self-regulation. To be well regulated, students require well-developed executive functions, as these provide the cognitive control mechanisms that underpin self-regulation (Zelazo & Carlson, 2012). For instance, a child resisting the impulse to call out in class is drawing on inhibitory control (an executive function) in the service of behavioural self-regulation. Similarly, a student persisting with a challenging maths problem relies on working memory to hold and manipulate information, while simultaneously self-regulating to sustain motivation and manage frustration. In everyday contexts, executive functions operate through self-regulation to help learners pursue goals and adapt to challenges – they are, in effect, the cognitive control supports. Within the classroom, there is both a pressing need and a rich opportunity to foster these capacities simultaneously.

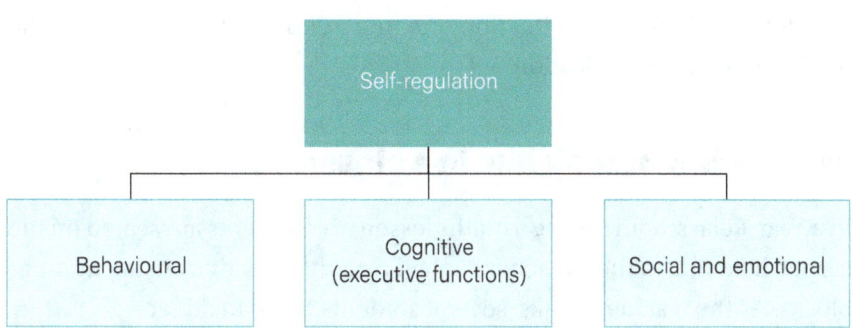

Figure 5: The components of self-regulation

From a neurobiological perspective, this mutual interdependence can be attributed to the neural interconnectivity between brain areas involved in emotional regulation (such as the amygdala in the limbic system) and those involved in behavioural and cognitive regulation (such as the prefrontal cortex) (Edossa et al., 2018). In the classroom, there is both a need and an opportunity to develop all three aspects simultaneously.

The *capacity* to self-regulate may be quite different from the reality. Just because a student *can* self-regulate doesn't mean that they *always will*. A student's ability to self-regulate may be different in different contexts. This is due to the various emotions and expectations that are associated with different contexts. It helps us understand what we are seeing in schools: the student who can concentrate for hours when they have a paintbush in their hand yet cannot focus for more than five minutes in a writing lesson.

As the name suggests, *self*-regulation entails regulation by oneself (intrinsic), as opposed to being regulated by others. In the SOWATT model the executive function *inhibitory control* is included under the self-regulation label. Inhibitory control refers to the ability to control automatic or dominant reactions, i.e. to stop, think, *then* act.

Delaying gratification is also part of self-regulation, and in a world geared for instant gratification, it can be difficult – even for adults. We all know the difficulty in resisting the urge to check our phones in response to the 'ding' of a text message or get our chocolate fix when we are trying to cut down on our sugar intake! Like inhibitory control, one major factor hindering its mastery is that it is closely linked to our emotions. The more emotionally charged the situation, the more difficult it is to suppress the desire for instant gratification.

What it might look like in a classroom

In a Year 1 classroom during a maths lesson, the students are seated on the carpet, listening to their teacher explain a counting activity using number blocks. As the teacher speaks, several students begin to fidget.

Tommy rolls onto his side, poking the student next to him and giggling loudly. Mia repeatedly interrupts the teacher with unrelated questions

about lunchtime. At the back of the group, Levi grabs a handful of number blocks from a nearby tray and begins stacking them noisily, ignoring the teacher's instruction to put them away.

A few other children start to lose focus, watching the disruptions instead of the teacher's demonstration. The lesson slows as the teacher pauses multiple times to redirect attention and ask for listening.

The classroom atmosphere grows increasingly unsettled, with some students becoming frustrated by the noise and others following the off-task behaviour.

However, the good news for teachers is that the skills needed to self-regulate can be fostered and taught directly with the use of various strategies and practices (Timmons et al., 2016).

SOWATT can teachers do?

Mindset and Motivation

(Why learning strategies matter and how to get students engaged)

- **Explain** to the students **why** this skill is important.
- **Reinforce positive actions** when a student successfully regulates behaviour or emotions; this boosts confidence and motivation.
- **Praise** *effort and persistence* over the end product. Praise students when they use coping or persevering strategies effectively.
- **Find the fun!**

Environmental and Structural Supports

(Creating classroom environments and routines that promote self-regulation and minimise dysregulation)

- **Model the desired behaviour.** Teachers should model self-regulation themselves. Children learn by observing the adults around them. Demonstrating how to handle frustration or disappointment calmly can be very powerful.
- **Have clear, consistent behaviour expectations.** Involve students in creating classroom rules to boost ownership and motivation.

- **Create a designated calm-down area** with stress-relief tools or visual prompts. These can be a great way to give students who really struggle to regulate their emotions a safe place to calm down when they are overwhelmed. This can include stress-relief toys or visual tools like 'calm-down' charts that guide students through breathing or relaxation exercises.
- **Prepare for transitions** with time checks. Giving time checks prior to changing activities can help to manage expectations and avoid emotional dysregulation.
- **Plan for breaks and downtime** (stretch breaks, individual breaks). Sometimes, students just need a break to reset. Constantly monitor your students for signs of fatigue or disengagement and intervene before negative behaviour escalates. It may be as simple as a whole-class 'stretch break' or allowing an individual to step away from a stressful situation or environment.
- **Establish routines for activities** (roles in group work, summarising group thinking). Assigning specific roles within group tasks, such as reporter, on-task manager, note-taker, timekeeper, etc., helps to keep students accountable and 'on task'.
- **Set an appropriate level of challenge** in activities (ZPD approach). If it's too easy, students get bored; if it's too difficult, students become frustrated – both can quickly lead to students becoming dysregulated. The ZPD is optimal, and this requires regular checking in with, and observations of, students while working.

Teaching and Learning Strategies

(Explicit instruction and practice of self-regulation skills)

- **Establish help-seeking routines** for students. Design and agree upon signals to access help or gain the teacher's attention that don't include calling out. The aim is not only to improve social interactions, but also to encourage students to 'sit with a problem' to build persistence – you will know which students need your help more than others.
- **Encourage goal setting.** Students can learn self-regulation by setting small, achievable goals for themselves. For instance, a goal could

be staying focused on a task for 10 minutes or waiting their turn during group activities. Regular goal setting teaches children to plan, evaluate and adjust their behaviour.

- **Turn and talk.** Set short (timed), focused, peer-to-peer conversations to discuss a part of the lesson – this may or may not involve reporting back to the class. This routine is highly effective because it engages multiple components of executive functioning inhibitory control, working memory, cognitive flexibility and metacognitive awareness.
- **Use TAPPLE** – **T**each first, **A**sk a question, **P**ause and pair-share, **P**ick a random volunteer, **L**isten to the response, **E**ffective feedback.
- **Teach the 'Pause and Plan' strategy.** This can encourage students to stop and think before acting. **Pause:** Encourage the student to take a deep breath or count to five when they start to feel upset. **Plan:** After pausing, they can decide what their next step is – whether to take a break, ask for help or reframe their thinking. This can be supported by a simple **visual prompt** (like a stop sign) to remind students to pause before reacting.
- **Teach social-emotional learning (SEL) skills.** Implementing SEL curricula helps children recognise and understand their emotions, practise empathy, manage relationships and develop social problem-solving skills. Integrating SEL into the daily curriculum strengthens students' emotional intelligence and self-regulation.
- **Develop emotional vocabulary.** Helping students label and express their emotions is a critical step in self-regulation. Use books, stories or games to teach students about emotions and how to articulate how they are feeling. This can help them recognise emotions before they get overwhelmed.
- **Teach conflict-management and problem-solving skills.** Conflict-resolution scripts are useful and readily available to support this. Once a student is more regulated following a meltdown, help them identify what caused the dysregulation and explore possible solutions. For example, if frustration was triggered by a difficult task, work together to break it down into smaller, manageable steps.
- **Use 'energy-release' activities.** Sometimes, students need to release pent-up energy to reset. Guide them through short, age-appropriate

activities designed to help them get their energy out in a constructive way; for example, Animal Movements: Have them perform animal-themed movements (for example, frog jumps, bear crawls or butterfly stretches) to release tension and get some exercise; or have a Dance Party: A three- to five-minute dance party can be a fun way for students to release pent-up energy.

- **Practise delayed gratification.** Encourage activities where students must wait for something they want. For example, give them a choice to earn a reward after completing a task or engaging in a productive activity. Games that require taking turns or waiting for a reward also promote this skill.
- **Incorporate mindfulness and relaxation techniques.** Teach students mindfulness exercises and regularly incorporate them into your practice. Techniques such as Box Breathing, meditation or guided imagery can help students increase their self-awareness, manage their emotions and improve their focus. Simple activities like 'belly breathing' or colouring can calm the mind and body. Also, 'oil and water calm jars' provide a good concrete example for younger students to use to help them understand the idea that our brains need to be calm in order to learn.

SOWATT can students do?

- Students need to develop awareness of the situations or factors that may trigger their dysregulation and have personalised strategies in their toolkit that work for them. Teachers can support this by explicitly teaching these strategies, providing opportunities to practise them and gradually reducing scaffolding so that students can use them independently.
- Know how to calmly communicate their needs. Even the most effective teacher can't read minds; students need to be encouraged to speak up when they need help or are feeling overwhelmed. OR – they need to establish clear and easy-to-use systems, like a visual cue or signal.

SOWATT can parents do?

- Establish routines – particularly in the morning, when all family members will be preparing for the day ahead, and at bedtime when energy and patience can be running low.
- Don't be a lawnmower parent, who goes to great lengths to remove all obstacles or difficulties from their child's path, often 'mowing down' challenges before the child even encounters them. Characteristics include: pre-emptively solving problems for their child instead of allowing them to handle it; intervening with teachers, coaches or peers to avoid discomfort or failure; micromanaging situations to ensure their child's success or comfort; preventing the child from learning resilience, problem solving or independence.
- Establish clear guidelines around interrupting or talking over other family members.
- Have fair, consistent behaviour expectations and follow through on consequences if the expectations are not met.
- Understand the concept of 'autonomy support' – the idea of giving 'just enough' support, starting with verbal cues and only physically helping your child to do something as a last resort.
- Play board and card games that require turn taking. Don't let children win to avoid meltdowns – they need to be able to have these in the comfort of their home and learn to deal with them in a very supportive environment.
- Get children active and limit use of passive screentime.

> **Joke:**
> "I seriously need a speedbump between my brain and my mouth!"

My summary

What are your key takeaways?

How does this chapter relate to what you already know or do?

Chapter 4

Organisation

"You do not rise to the level of your goals. You fall to the level of your systems"

– James Clear

Organisation refers to:

- Classroom management
- Goal setting
- Time – routines, transitions
- Space – layout of classroom and personal space
- Resources – shared and personal belongings
- Ideas – planning and prioritising
- Information

Why is it important?

Organisation is an important concept to develop in our primary school students because it lays the foundation for independence, responsibility and effective learning. When students learn to organise their time, resources and ideas, they're better able to focus, follow instructions and complete activities successfully. Organised students are less likely to feel overwhelmed or forget important steps, which helps build confidence and reduces stress. From a cognitive perspective, organisation also supports memory by helping the brain sort and store information in a more structured way, making it easier to recall later. These skills don't just support academic success, they also prepare students to navigate everyday life with greater ease, from packing their school bag to planning a project.

What it might look like in a classroom

The bell rings to signal the start of the day, and Mr Pollard's Year 5 class begins to file in. While most students quickly unpack their bags, place their diaries on their desks and get started on the morning warm-up, a few are already falling behind.

Liam can't find his pencil case. He left it somewhere yesterday, but he's not sure where. Emily forgot her homework folder again and has no idea what's due. Meanwhile, Noah hasn't finished yesterday's activity because he lost track of time during independent work. As the rest of the class moves on to the next task, these students scramble to catch up, missing instructions and falling further behind.

In contrast, Sophie opens her planner to check the day's timetable, retrieves the materials she needs from her clearly labelled trays and calmly begins her morning task. She knows that maths comes next and has already set out her workbook and ruler. Because she's organised her time, belongings and resources, she's able to focus, participate confidently and help others when needed.

This simple morning snapshot shows how good organisational skills support smoother transitions, reduce stress and create more time for learning. The school day runs on a predictable rhythm: timetables, bells, breaks and lessons – all underpinned by a finely tuned system that quietly keeps everything running smoothly. Yet many students struggle to follow this system and need support to navigate it successfully.

For students, organisation isn't just about keeping their books in order or remembering where their diary is. It's about being ready to learn. From the moment the bell rings, students are expected to switch gears, follow

instructions and manage their belongings and time. Teachers rely on this shared structure to maximise learning time and reduce disruptions. Schools, too, depend on predictable routines to coordinate everything from specialist classes to recess duty.

When students develop strong organisational habits, such as packing their bags the night before, checking the timetable and arriving on time, they are better prepared to engage in learning. And when these habits are modelled, supported and practised throughout the school day, they lay the groundwork for independence and success, both in and beyond the classroom.

SOWATT can teachers do?

Discuss what students understand by the term 'organised' and ask them why it is important.

One way to support the development of organisational skills is to draw attention to how things are organised in the real world. Society has designed systems dedicated to organisation; from the multistorey carpark to the dishwasher, we are surrounded by cues that help to make our lives more structured, efficient and ultimately easier.

Classroom management

Effective classroom management is proactive, consistent and fair. It begins with clearly establishing rules and expectations at the start of the school year. While the word *rules* can carry negative connotations, it doesn't have to. At their core, rules are about keeping ourselves and others safe within the communities we belong to. In the classroom, rules should also be designed to support the learning process. Framing them in this way encourages metacognitive development by prompting students to reflect on the reasons behind each rule.

Whenever possible, involve students in creating the rules. This promotes ownership and deeper understanding; just be sure to keep the language positive and limit the list to five or six key rules. If you are stuck, or looking for inspiration, consider using the six Ps: Be Prompt, Prepared, Productive, Polite, Patient and Proud. These would obviously need to be unpacked for your context, but once agreed upon, consistency is crucial. Like routines, consistent rules reduce anxiety and provide the external structure children need to organise their behaviour, creating the ideal conditions for internalising self-regulation strategies.

Goal setting

For primary students to set effective goals, they need to be explicitly taught and given multiple opportunities to practise. It is not simply a matter of students stating something that they may want to achieve by the end of the term/year. It involves breaking down the process into manageable, clear and engaging steps. Since primary-aged students are still developing their understanding of time, planning and self-regulation, it's important to make goal setting both motivating and meaningful. Supporting students to achieve this could include **starting with simple, achievable goals**.

Large, abstract goals not only feel overwhelming, they serve very little purpose and find themselves in the realm of 'dreams' rather than goals. Focus instead on small, achievable goals that students can fairly easily see themselves accomplishing. Remember that motivation usually comes with accomplishment, not the other way around. For example, instead of saying, "I want to get better at maths", a student might set the goal, "I will complete five maths problems every day this week". Make sure the goals are specific, measurable and realistic for their level of development.

There are several frameworks to help with goal setting. One commonly used is SMART, with five steps that need to be addressed. Focusing on these aspects, students can set goals that feel manageable, and they'll have a clearer idea of how to work towards achieving them.

- **Specific:** Ask, "What exactly do I want to achieve?" (For example, "I want to improve my reading skills by reading one new book each week.")
- **Measurable:** Ask, "How will I know I've succeeded?" (For example, "I will finish five chapters by the end of the week.")
- **Achievable:** Ask, "Is it something I can realistically do?" (For example, "I can read for 15 minutes each day.")

- **Relevant:** Ask, "Why is this goal important to me?" (For example, "I want to get better at reading so I can read *Harry Potter*.")
- **Time-bound:** Ask, "When do I want to achieve this?" (For example, "I'll aim to complete my goal by Friday.")

Another acronym used for goal setting is DART: Detailed, Achievable, Realistic and Time-based:

- **Direction:** Be clear about *where you're headed* – what exactly is the desired outcome?
- **Action:** Identify the *specific steps* or behaviours needed to move towards the goal.
- **Review:** Regularly *monitor progress*, reflect on what's working and make adjustments as needed.
- **Timeline:** Set a realistic *timeframe* or deadline to create urgency and keep momentum.

Students are more likely to engage with their goals if they feel a sense of ownership over them (autonomy). Encourage them to set their own goals or at least be involved in the goal-setting process. Additionally, encourage students to reflect on their goals regularly. Build in opportunities for students to regularly check in with themselves at the end of the week or month.

Primary students are often more engaged when they can see their progress. Creating visual goal-tracking systems like a goal chart, a progress bar or stickers that they can add each time they make progress can be motivating for many students. For example, if their goal is to complete five reading activities in a week, they could colour in a box for each activity they finish. This makes the process interactive, visible and more rewarding, especially when small successes are celebrated along the way.

It is also important to teach children that not every goal will be easily achieved, and that setbacks are part of the learning process. Encourage students to keep trying even if things don't go as planned and celebrate the effort as much as the outcome. This builds resilience and helps students learn that working towards a goal is just as important as achieving it. Draw inspiration from favourite or well-known sports stars, authors or celebrities who have experienced significant setbacks on their journeys. Two examples who come readily to mind are J. K. Rowling and David Beckham.

Although goal setting is frequently associated with aims that may need time to achieve, don't neglect the short-term goals that can be achieved in a single lesson. From the teacher's perspective, this is usually referred to as the 'Learning Intention' for the lesson. From a student perspective, it may be as simple as using a 'Plan, Do, Check' routine.

Having communal, whole-class conversations about goal setting creates a culture of improvement and encourages a growth mindset in students that fosters cooperation and mutual improvement. We all get better when each of us gets better, which reminds me, don't forget to share YOUR goal – model the process and share the challenges you face along the way to achieving it!

Depending on the age of the students, an approach that may be worth exploring is to pair them up to help one another with goal setting and monitoring. Importantly, peer partnerships need to be thoughtfully managed to ensure compatibility, equity and positive dynamics, but when successful, they cultivate a classroom culture where students actively support one another's growth in executive functioning and self-regulation.

An alternative to goal setting is **making a pact**. According to Anne-Laure Le Cunff (2025), the difference between a goal and a pact is that rather than being outcome-focused, a pact is a commitment to a process or behaviour. It is 'present-focused and action-oriented'. Allegedly, pacts are more effective for building habits because they reduce the pressure of a distant, possibly overwhelming outcome and instead focus on consistent, manageable action. For example, rather than setting the goal *"I will finish three chapter books by the end of the term"*, a student might create a pact: *"Every afternoon after lunch, I will read quietly for 10 minutes and share one thing I noticed with my partner."* The focus here is not on the distant result but on the daily process, which builds sustainable habits. Pacts reportedly promote intrinsic motivation and reduce procrastination, as they are tied to identity and values rather than just outcomes. As teachers, we want our students to develop good habits, especially if the aim is to

support them to become better learners. To that end, I say, use what works for you and your students, and don't get too hung up on the semantics!

Organising time

This is a critical aspect of organisation. Structures that support classroom organisation should be evident and consistent. Having set schedules helps students know not just what to expect and plan accordingly but reduces any anxiety about what might be coming next. Teachers can encourage children to create their own schedules or 'to-do lists', gradually helping them internalise time-management skills.

Work on creating effective classroom transitions, such as moving from group activities to independent work, as these moments place high demands on children's executive functions. Shifting from one task to another requires inhibition (stopping the current activity), cognitive flexibility (adapting to the new expectation) and working memory (holding the next set of instructions in mind).

Teachers can support this by explicitly teaching and rehearsing routines that make transitions predictable and efficient. For example, use clear visual or auditory signals to mark the end of an activity and provide short reminders of what comes next. Break the process into manageable steps: *"First, pack away materials, then collect your notebook, then sit at your desk"* to reduce cognitive load and support working memory.

Time-management strategies can also be embedded into transitions. For younger students, sand timers, countdowns or music cues help them pace their actions. Older students can benefit from checklists or planners that reinforce self-monitoring and organisation. Importantly, teachers should model the desired behaviours, narrating the process aloud to show how to plan and sequence actions.

When transitions are smooth, the classroom atmosphere becomes calmer and instructional time is maximised. Over time, students internalise these habits, enabling them to move between tasks with growing independence and minimal distraction.

The majority of students will benefit from teachers explicitly teaching them how to organise and manage their time. In the upper primary classes, where tasks such as project-based learning may extend over a longer period of time, it cannot be assumed that all students will be able to do this.

To support students organise their time, you can:

- Use **starter activity routines** that students are expected to do quickly and independently at the start of a lesson. Have clear expectations of what the start of a lesson looks like, for example, all necessary resources ready and students sitting down. This could include the use of a timer, which provides a good visual reminder.
- Establish clear **routines for the end of the day**. Provide time for students to pack their bags before being dismissed, as this sends the message that you value organisation and that you are available to support the students you know will struggle to do this task thoroughly, which reduces their stress levels.
- Use **checklists** and get students to tick things off as they are completed – this creates a mini dopamine hit and builds motivation.
- Use **visual schedules** and colour code them for easy understanding. Remind students to refer to them regularly.
- Provide **time prompts** prior to transitions – this helps to manage expectations.
- Get students to use a diary/calendar to keep track of homework and when long assignments are due.

A **visual timer** can help students with time management, transitions and knowing when they will be able to return to a task. For example:

- If they are taking a break, a visual timer lets students see how long they have before they need to return to class activities. This helps reduce anxiety about the unknown.
- It's also a great tool for students who have difficulty understanding the passage of time.

Organising space

This is another area where students can benefit from instruction and good modelling. After all, there is no point insisting on clutter-free student desks if your own looks as though it hasn't been touched in six months! A cluttered classroom or personal workspace can be both overwhelming and distracting. Teaching students the importance of a tidy and functional space using simple practices, like keeping materials in designated areas, using storage boxes or folders and ensuring that workspaces are clear of unnecessary items, can greatly improve concentration and efficiency. A similar routine might be applied to personal backpacks and lockers. These activities lend themselves to a peer-to-peer format in which students have a partner and they help each other complete the steps in the process.

Organising resources

Both shared and personal resources also require careful organisation. Whether it's textbooks, art supplies or shared computers, it is important to teach students how to use and respect communal resources, and to keep their workspace orderly. This is key to developing responsibility. Students also need to learn how to keep track of their personal belongings, such as their clothes or school supplies. To support students to organise their resources, ask them to label personal possessions with their full name, and colour code folders for different subjects. This reduces the potential chaos, even meltdown, that can occur when items go missing and is especially important for primary students who are still developing their sense of responsibility and accountability.

Organising ideas

Alongside time management, primary students also need to learn how to organise their ideas. Whether they are organising their thoughts for a writing project, deciding which books to read or figuring out the best way to solve a maths problem, students need strategies for sorting through their ideas. Teachers can support this by introducing brainstorming exercises, mind maps and other graphic organisers that help students make their thinking visible – not only to themselves, but to the teacher.

Planning and prioritising tasks are key elements in developing organisational skills. Together, they empower students to approach tasks with intention rather than reactively, reducing anxiety and increasing their sense of control. These skills also foster independence, responsibility and self-confidence as students begin to internalise routines, manage multistep tasks and see the results of their efforts. They are particularly important when students work on more open-ended tasks, such as inquiry projects. Without a clear plan and the ability to prioritise tasks, students can easily become overwhelmed, distracted or disengaged.

Many students do not see the need for planning and consider it a waste of time. My own daughter, a gifted writer, would never plan her stories (in spite of encouragement!), arguing that she preferred to "just write". Gradually, as assignments became more complex, the need to plan became more obvious to her. However, if planning is introduced in the primary school years, it becomes the norm, rather than the exception.

Don't forget to model planning behaviour and make lists of steps for a project together.

Organising information

Another essential skill for learning is the organisation of information. From taking notes to sorting through research, students need strategies for managing the vast amounts of information they encounter daily. Using folders, notebooks and digital tools can help them organise facts, ideas and notes, so they can find what they need quickly and effectively.

Teaching the layout of non-fiction texts explicitly gives students a roadmap for understanding and using information. Many non-fiction features are not consciously noticed by students, especially younger learners or those with limited exposure to informational texts. Explicit teaching demystifies the structure and helps students realise that the way information is presented is intentional and purposeful. It encourages students to use those features strategically when reading, writing or researching. When students understand the structure of non-fiction texts, they become more independent learners. They are able to skim and scan for key facts, use the table of contents or index to find information efficiently and take notes from specific sections without having to read the entire book.

Teaching students how to set their work out neatly is not just about appearance – it's a powerful way to support thinking, learning and communication. When students set out their work clearly with headings, spacing and structure, it helps them organise their thoughts more effectively, break tasks into steps and see relationships between ideas (for example, in maths, writing or science). When work is neat, students spend less time searching for where they left off, it's easier to spot and fix mistakes and the brain can focus on the content and not the clutter, which reduces cognitive overload, especially for students with learning differences or attention challenges.

Note-taking is a useful skill to start developing with upper primary students. It is less about polished summaries and more about giving them tools to organise and process information effectively. Introduce simple structures to scaffold the process. This could include:

- **Bullet points:** listing key facts in short form.
- **T-charts:** dividing information into categories (for example, causes/effects).
- **Mind maps:** linking ideas visually to show relationships.
- **Cornell notes (simplified):** with a section for main ideas, details and a summary.

Practise together at first – provide content and guide students in deciding what to capture. Then move to guided practice where they try independently, followed by sharing and comparing strategies as a class. Encourage them to use colour coding, symbols or drawings to personalise their notes, reinforcing that organisation can be both visual and verbal.

Finally, make note-taking purposeful. Show students how notes can be used later for revision, group discussion or project planning. This reinforces the value of the process, not just the product, and helps them see note-taking as a tool for learning rather than just another task. Over time, students develop confidence and independence in organising information in ways that support their memory, focus and understanding.

Remember to find the fun in organisation!

SOWATT can parents do?

- Label their child's school supplies and clothing.
- Encourage their child to pack their school bag the night before, when there are less time pressures on the morning routine.
- Model the use of calendars to schedule after-school activities and fun activities.
- Create consistent routines, which might include:
  - Morning and bedtime routines
  - Homework time
  - A regular spot in the house for backpacks and shoes
- Stand back and let their child do things for themselves, even if they struggle and tasks, such as packing the school bag, take longer initially. It really is a question of 'short-term pain for long-term gain'.
- Involve their child in household chores – make a schedule for the whole family and assign specific jobs with timeframes. Younger children may require an adult to co-organise while they learn the ropes. Include tasks that involve sorting or classifying. We tend to recall things by groups or concepts, but children need to learn them first.
- Offer choices and let their child practise organising:
  - "Would you like to do homework before or after your snack?"
  - "How do you want to organise your bedroom?"
- Help their child prioritise tasks – this could be based on urgency, difficulty or the level of stress they have about the tasks.
- Monitor screen usage, talk about deadlines and, if required, provide prompts for deadlines.
- Cook together – this teaches planning, following directions, sequencing, impulse control, managing time and, of course, delay of gratification.
- Praise effort, not perfection!

Joke:

"I'm trying to organise a hide-and-seek tournament, but good players are really hard to find."

My summary

What are your key takeaways?

How does this chapter relate to what you already know or do?

Chapter 5

Working memory

"The true art of memory is the art of attention"

– Samuel Johnson

Working memory refers to:

The ability to hold information in your head long enough to use it.

Put simply, working memory is like the brain's Post-it note or mini whiteboard – it keeps important information active for a short time so we can use it.

From a neurological perspective, the prefrontal cortex works with the parts of the brain that process sights and sounds, helping us keep information in mind for a short time, even after we've stopped looking or listening (Rogers & Thomas, 2022). Classic experiments showed that unless we rehearse it, information vanishes from working memory in just a few seconds (Peterson & Peterson, 1959).

Working memory is closely linked to attention. The neural networks for the control of attention and working are largely overlapping (Zhou et al., 2022). To illustrate this, the following scenario may be familiar to some of you...

You go into the kitchen with the intention of doing something, but once you get there, you're not sure what it was that you wanted; you find yourself staring at the oven trying to remember what it was you were going to do. There was a clear instruction in your head a few moments earlier and now it has gone! Did you want to take something out of the fridge? Boil the kettle? Or look for your car keys? There's a chance that you were distracted by a ping from your mobile phone, or the dishes in the sink waiting to be washed. Perhaps you were already planning what you were going to eat that evening. Whatever it was, the outcome was a surplus of information in your brain that left you standing staring at the oven!

Figure 6 explains how the human brain processes and stores information, highlighting the limitations of working memory, the process of learning and the role of long-term memory.

The human brain can only process a small amount of new information at once. That is why working memory is sometimes described as the "bottleneck of our thinking" (Lovell, 2020). Learning occurs when information moves from the working memory into the long-term memory. This is the key transition – if information isn't transferred, it is forgotten. While working memory is limited, long-term memory can handle a vast amount of information efficiently. This explains why repetition and consolidation are key to learning. One of the ways our brain manages this transfer and organisation of information is through schemas.

Schemas play a huge role in learning because they're how our brains organise and store knowledge. They help reduce the cognitive load, support faster processing, and enable us to transfer learning and build understanding over time. You can think of a schema as a mental framework, or a blueprint, that helps you organise and make sense of information. It's like having a folder on your computer where you keep related documents together.

Figure 6: Working memory in the human brain

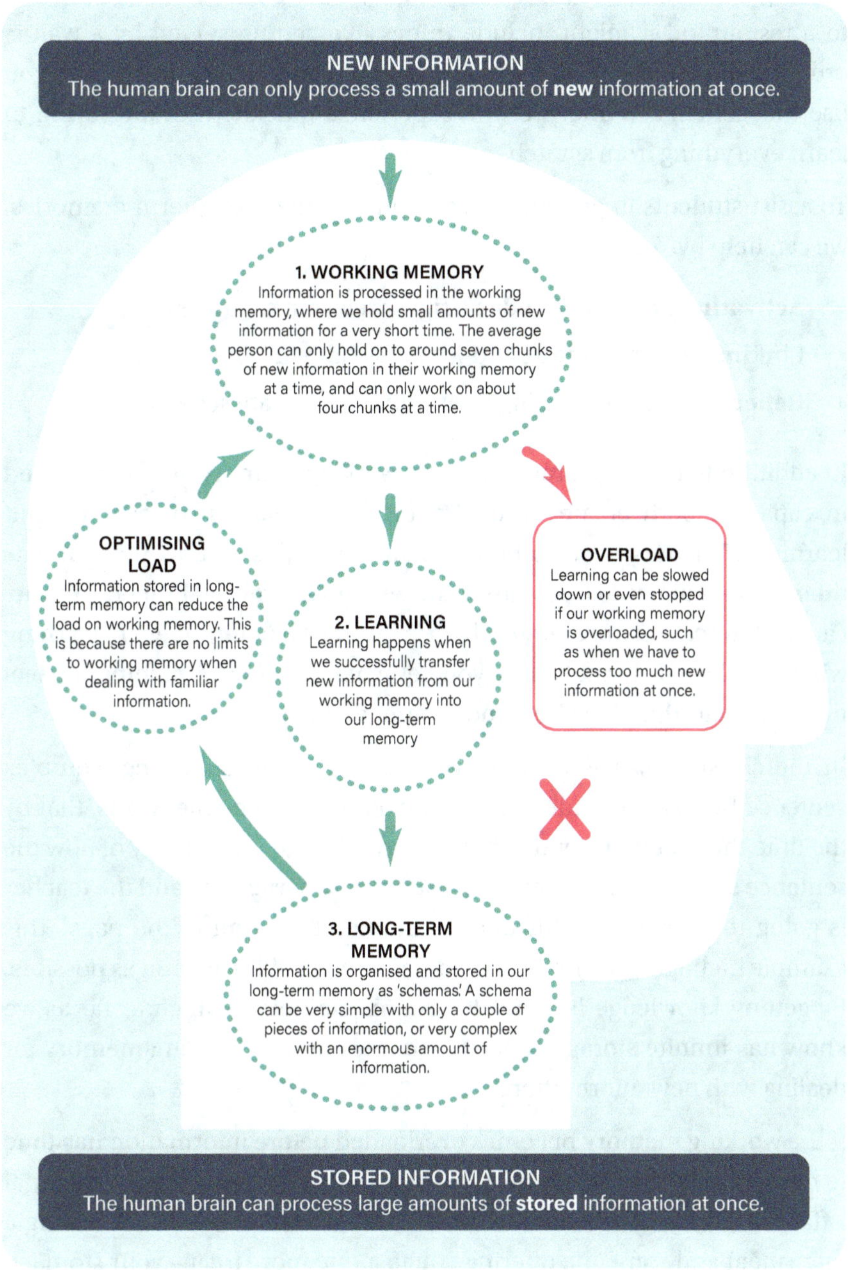

NEW INFORMATION
The human brain can only process a small amount of **new** information at once.

1. WORKING MEMORY
Information is processed in the working memory, where we hold small amounts of new information for a very short time. The average person can only hold on to around seven chunks of new information in their working memory at a time, and can only work on about four chunks at a time.

OPTIMISING LOAD
Information stored in long-term memory can reduce the load on working memory. This is because there are no limits to working memory when dealing with familiar information.

2. LEARNING
Learning happens when we successfully transfer new information from our working memory into our long-term memory

OVERLOAD
Learning can be slowed down or even stopped if our working memory is overloaded, such as when we have to process too much new information at once.

3. LONG-TERM MEMORY
Information is organised and stored in our long-term memory as 'schemas'. A schema can be very simple with only a couple of pieces of information, or very complex with an enormous amount of information.

STORED INFORMATION
The human brain can process large amounts of **stored** information at once.

© New South Wales Department of Education (2018)

When we encounter new information, our brain tries to fit it into these existing 'folders' or schemas. For example, if you have a schema for 'going to a restaurant', it might include things like getting served by a waiter, ordering food and paying the bill. When you go to a new restaurant, you use this schema to interpret the experience quickly, without having to learn everything from scratch.

To assist students in getting information into their long-term memories, we can help by:

- **Activating prior knowledge** (trigger relevant schemas)
- **Linking new information** to what they already know
- **Reflecting** on and revising their thinking (update schemas)

In addition to the temporary nature of working memory, it is also limited in capacity. Both elements are important in relation to teaching and learning. Teachers need to be as cognisant of this fact, as the students themselves. Failure to be aware of the working memory's limited capacity can lead to *cognitive overload*, which is saturation point, when no learning will take place. It's that feeling you get when you start switching off, feel tired and start thinking about more immediate needs.

In the classroom, it is evident when a student reads a long, complex sentence but has expended so much energy decoding the words, that by the time they get to the end of it, they have little or no memory of how the sentence started. This sentence is just one in a paragraph, and the teacher is going to be checking for understanding at the end of the page! This example highlights the need to automatise basic skills as soon as possible. By getting knowledge into our long-term memory – which as far as we know has infinite storage capacity – it frees up our working memory for dealing with new information.

If the working memory becomes overloaded before information has time to move into long-term memory, learning is interrupted and new material is far less likely to be retained. Using a food metaphor, it's like eating a huge meal and someone offering you just one more treat – your stomach simply can't take any more; even a small bite would tip you over the edge. Cognitive overload is the brain's equivalent – when your working memory

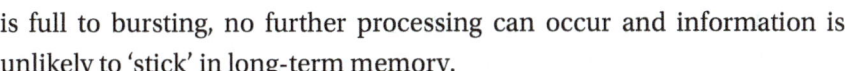

is full to bursting, no further processing can occur and information is unlikely to 'stick' in long-term memory.

Cognitive load theory (CLT) is a framework that helps us understand how the human brain processes and stores information, particularly when learning new concepts. It was developed by John Sweller in the 1980s, and it's particularly relevant in educational contexts, such as primary school classrooms. From a teacher's perspective, it helps us work out how best to use the limited learning resource that constrains all human thinking (Lovell, 2020). An understanding of the theory can help teachers support students to become more successful and independent learners.

Cognitive load can be broken down into two components: *intrinsic load* and *extraneous load*.

1. **Intrinsic load**

    This is the load that is associated with the core learning taking place. For example, if a student is learning to read, being able to connect letters and sounds would be the intrinsic goal – there is no way round it. Therefore, this is what we want the working memory to be used for. It is based on the task's complexity and the learner's prior knowledge. It includes effort devoted to schema construction and automation. The teaching goal is to manage it by:

    - Sequencing tasks from simple to complex
    - Chunking information
    - Scaffolding complex tasks
    - Activating prior knowledge before introducing new content

2. **Extraneous load**

    This is imposed by *the way the material is presented* or any irrelevant task demands that do *not* support learning. It draws students' working memory away from the core information to be learned. Exactly what is – or isn't – extraneous load will depend on the learning intentions of the lesson. However, teachers should try and minimise this by:

    - Improving their instructional design – for example, by avoiding unnecessary details such as slides or worksheets with cluttered layouts that splits students' attention

- Using clear visuals paired with concise verbal explanations
- Designing tasks with minimal irrelevant processing

The bottom line is that learning is most effective when the *essential cognitive effort* (intrinsic load) is carefully managed, and *unnecessary mental effort* (extraneous load) is minimised. This allows the working memory to work on building and strengthening schemas.

Intrinsic load + extraneous load must NOT exceed the capacity of the working memory!

Examples of intrinsic load in the classroom:

- Reading a new phonics pattern (Year 1), for example, the 'igh' trigraph
    - Students must understand that groups of certain letters can make just one sound and have previous experience with digraphs.
    - It requires being able to recognise patterns by looking for several examples of 'igh' in context – light, night, fight.
- Understanding the water cycle (Years 3–4)
    - Concepts like evaporation, condensation and precipitation are abstract for younger learners.
    - It requires an understanding of sequential processes and scientific vocabulary.
- Learning long division (Years 4–6)
    - Students must understand place value, subtraction, multiplication and division all at once.
    - The task is inherently complex for beginners due to multiple steps and decision points.

Examples of extraneous load in the classroom:

- Cluttered worksheets
    - A maths worksheet that includes excessive clipart, fancy fonts and unnecessary borders. These visual elements distract from solving the equations, increasing cognitive load.
- Ineffective instructions

- A teacher gives multistep instructions verbally and quickly without any visuals or repetition, which leaves students struggling to remember the steps rather than focusing on the task itself.
- Unclear learning objectives
  - A science lesson jumps between unrelated facts without a clear structure or focus, leaving students to spend effort trying to make sense of what they're supposed to learn.
- Using a complicated app for simple tasks
  - Using a flashy interactive whiteboard tool with too many animations to teach basic spelling. The tool overwhelms students and shifts attention away from the spelling words.

SOWATT can teachers do?

Mindset and Motivation

(Why learning strategies matter and getting students engaged)

- **Explain that for new learning to stick, information needs to move from working memory into long-term memory**, where it can be stored and retrieved later. This transfer doesn't happen automatically – it requires active engagement, such as thinking about, organising or practising the material.
- **Explain the limited capacity of working memory** to students and, therefore, the need to pay attention when instructions are given.
- **Be aware of CLT** and explain its relevance to students.
- **View tests as a vehicle for learning.** Since tests require information to be retrieved from the long-term memory, they are a good way of finding out how much has been learned or understood. When students take more low-stakes tests, they get more familiar with what they are having difficulty with, and so does the teacher! Framing tests in the positive allows for students to recognise the need to change their approach to learning to make information stick. Alongside testing, teachers need to teach students how to 'test themselves'. This can include activities that require students to retrieve or

generate information, for example, using flashcards to practise vocabulary, rather than just representing information to themselves.
- **Find the fun!**

Environmental and Structural Supports

(Organising tasks, instructions and learning environments to reduce overload)

- **Simplify instructions.** Present information in small, manageable chunks. This helps reduce intrinsic load and ensures students can absorb one thing at a time.
- **Be aware of the level of background noise** – this can add to extraneous load (see the section on CLT on page 73).
- **Give prompts and reminders before starting new activities.** Remind students what you want them to focus on when doing an activity.
- **Automatise basic routines and information**, for example, the morning routine: how you want workbooks to be set out, letter formation, letter sounds, friends of 10, doubles facts and multiplication tables.
- **Scaffold tasks.** Scaffolds come in many shapes and sizes depending on the task. In literacy they might involve sentence starters or a graphic organiser to plan a story, whereas in an inquiry unit, it might be an exemplar of a poster which you can use with students to highlight the key elements and their relative sizing.
- **Use graphic organisers** to teach new concepts and show relationships between ideas. When students can picture how the ideas are interrelated, they can be stored and retrieved more easily.
- **Deliberately provide opportunities for students to retrieve information.** Learning becomes accessible, flexible and usable only when knowledge is actively retrieved and temporarily held in working memory.

Teaching and Learning Strategies

(Explicit strategies to support memory, thinking and self-regulation during learning)

- **Use worked examples.** This is a particularly useful skill to employ when teaching maths. There is less burden on the working memory when new material is practised using worked examples. Instead of focusing solely on the answer to the problem, students are able to focus on how to solve it. Using worked examples allows for a narration of the thought process; this has the added benefit of supporting students' metacognition and self-regulation. It makes the implicit explicit, thereby reducing ambiguity and doubt.
- **Ask students to verbalise steps** when completing difficult tasks. This can provide important information about where a breakdown is occurring and what supports are likely to work best to fix it.
- **Encourage active engagement in learning**, for example, encouraging active reading by underlining or highlighting text can help students keep the information in mind long enough to answer questions about it. Summarise information/themes at the end of a chapter.
- **Talking out loud and asking questions** about the reading material helps to make links to prior knowledge.
- **Provide opportunities for students to organise information and connect new ideas to what they already know.** This helps deepen understanding and supports long-term retention.
- **Use checklists/acronyms for writing assignments**, for example, P.O.W.E.R for writing assignments (Plan, Organise, Write, Edit, Revise); P.E.N.S for sentence writing (Pick a formula, Explore the words, Note the words, Search and check); C.U.P.S for editing/proofreading writing (Capitalisation, Understanding, Punctuation, Spelling).
- **Use 'Pause, paraphrase, summarise'.** Stop at least twice in a lesson and request a quick summary from students; ask, "What have we learnt so far?"
- **Introduce the Rule of 3:** (work with, revisit and retrieve)

Work with the information (for example, discuss, practise or apply it in a new context).

Revisit and retrieve it later (for example, recall it from memory, explain it to someone else or use it in problem solving).

Each encounter should involve effortful thinking: making connections, asking questions or comparing it to what is already known, because it is this mental processing that strengthens the neural pathways for storage in the long-term memory. Without it, information may be briefly understood but quickly forgotten.

- **Use rhymes to aid memorisation**, for example, *"The water cycle goes round and round, evaporation, clouds, then rain comes down."*
- **Work on visualisation skills.** Encourage students to create a picture in their mind of what they've just read or heard. They can draw a picture of it or, as they get better at visualising, they can describe the image instead of drawing it.
- **Promote active recall** using a 3 x 3 grid: three rows and three columns, containing nine prompts, questions, keywords or concepts (see examples in the resources section on page 155).
- **Have the students teach/explain something to someone else.** Being able to explain how to do something involves making sense of information and mentally filing it. Pairing up students in class lets them start working with the information right away rather than waiting to be called on.

SOWATT can students do?

- Have an understanding of the limited capacity of working memory and the need to get knowledge into the long-term memory.
- Reduce the demands on the working memory by committing repetitive information to the long-term memory, for example, multiplication tables and high-frequency spelling words.
- Understand that cognitive load increases when switching between multiple tasks. Multitasking divides attention and reduces the brain's ability to process information efficiently.

- Ask 'why' or 'how' questions that help make meaningful links between new and prior knowledge.
- Practise self-testing and retrieval practice: actively recalling information (self-testing) strengthens memory and understanding, making it easier to retrieve in the future. This can be achieved by students:
    - Using flashcards to test their knowledge
    - Practising solving problems without looking at solutions
    - Quizzing themselves regularly on key concepts to reinforce learning
    - Prioritising understanding over memorisation by asking themselves 'why' and 'how' questions to understand the material more deeply
- Teaching the material to someone else (or pretending to).

SOWATT can parents do?

- Be aware of the number of instructions you give in one go.
- Make lists of jobs that need to be done at home and cross off things that have been completed.
- Talk out loud when solving a problem, for example, "Let's remember the steps. First, we…" Then encourage children to do the same.
- Play boardgames and card games that require remembering things and following rules.

> **Joke:**
>
> **Q:** What do you call a teacher who forgets to take attendance?
>
> **A:** Absentminded

Working memory

My summary

What are your key takeaways?

How does this chapter relate to what you already know or do?

Chapter 6

Attention

"Your focus determines your reality"
– Qui-Gon Jinn (*Star Wars: The Phantom Menace*)

Attention refers to the ability that allows us to focus on one person or task for a period of time. If we are not paying attention when there's something to be learned, then we won't learn it.

Attention is generally agreed to comprise of three components (Posner & Petersen, 1990):

- **Alertness** – can be too much (for example, attention deficit disorder) or too little (tired) and often linked to emotions/attitudes.
- **Orientation** – paying attention to the desired stimuli.
- **Executive/sustained attention** – requires effortful attention on the correct material.

The ability of a student to regulate their attentional resources is a critical skill for accessing learning, particularly in a group environment where there may be many things competing for their attention. From a teacher's perspective, the need to manage and engage students' attention has never been more critical. In our classrooms we are seeing a growing number of students diagnosed with attention-related challenges, therefore, teachers must be deliberate in designing learning experiences that capture focus, minimise distractions and support the development of self-regulation skills, so all students can actively engage and benefit from instruction.

It is worth remembering that the brain is always 'paying attention'. While we're not consciously aware of everything happening around us, the brain is constantly processing information, even when we're not actively focused on it. This is because the brain is always taking in sensory data: sounds, sights, smells, etc. and making sense of it.

What we pay attention to is often influenced by memory, curiosity and novelty. There is a tendency to use previous experiences to predict where you should pay attention, therefore, different environments create different expectations. If we have an interest in a subject or a person, or something is importance to us, we will tend to pay more attention.

It is generally agreed across behavioural and neuroscience research that attention is a limited resource. It is considered to be limited in *capacity* (we can only attend to a few things at once), *duration* (sustained attention fades over time) and *flexibility* (switching tasks reduces performance). Understanding attention as a finite resource helps explain why distractions, multitasking and cognitive overload reduce learning and performance. If teachers understand the different aspects of attention, we can begin to harness this vital ability more effectively.

Alertness

Alertness refers to students' state of mental readiness, focus and attentiveness during learning activities. When students are alert, they are more likely to be mentally engaged, actively processing information and capable of responding to the content being taught.

Alertness can be influenced by many factors, including sleep, hunger, nutrition, classroom emotional states and even the temperature of the classroom. Students who are well-rested are generally more alert than those who are tired (Curcio et al., 2006). Likewise, a classroom with low lighting, high noise level or uncomfortable seating may reduce students' alertness, making it harder for them to focus and retain information (McCoy & Evans, 2002). While this may seem obvious, it is often overlooked.

Orientation

Orientation refers to the initial phase of attention where students become mentally ready and focused on the learning task at hand. It involves the process of directing their cognitive resources towards the subject matter, setting aside distractions and becoming aware of the task or topic being presented. Essentially, orientation is the mental shift that students undergo to engage with the content of the lesson or activity. Attention is often likened to a beam of light or spotlight. In much the same way as you can aim a torch at a certain object in a darkened room, you can direct your attention at selected parts of your surroundings and choose a small amount of information from everything around you.

Something to be aware of is *'attention contagion'*. This is when one student's attention or focus spreads to others. In a classroom, this often happens when a few students focus on something they consider interesting or important, and that focus draws the attention of others. It's similar to how yawning or laughter can spread in a group. On the positive side, attention contagion can boost group focus and improve self-regulation, as students learn to manage their attention by watching how others focus. When the whole class pays attention to the same thing, it helps to build shared learning through collaboration and collective understanding (Frith & Frith, 2007). The flip side of this is if one or two students lose focus, start fidgeting, whispering or go off-task, others may quickly follow. The attention of the group can shift from learning to off-task behaviour, just as easily as it can shift towards learning. If a student is concentrating deeply but the group is distracted, it can be hard for them to stay focused. The social pressure to follow group attention can override their internal motivation. The implications of attention contagion for teachers is obvious; we need to actively guide students' attention using tools such as visual cues, strategic positioning (students and teacher) and engaging content.

Sustained attention

Sustained attention involves maintaining focus over time, which can be particularly challenging during long or less engaging lessons. It involves students resisting distractions, staying alert and managing cognitive resources to prevent mental fatigue. For instance, a student may be able to pay attention for a short burst of time when the teacher introduces a new topic, but they need sustained attention to continue following the lesson, processing information and retaining key concepts until the class is over.

In an ideal classroom, we would like our students to be in a state of 'flow', a term coined by Csíkszentmihályi and LeFevre (1989). It is a state of mind where a person is fully immersed in an activity, totally absorbed and energised by it, without being distracted by anything else. According to Csíkszentmihályi and LeFevre, we enter flow when there's a balance between the challenge of a task and our abilities to meet it, resulting in deep engagement and a sense of control (see the ZPD, as described in Chapter 3). This state is marked by high productivity, creativity and enjoyment, making it a crucial aspect of not only personal happiness, but also professional success and fulfilment.

Csíkszentmihályi and LeFevre identified several features that are common when someone is in flow:

- **Intense concentration** – you're fully focused on the task at hand, with no room for distractions.
- **Merging of action and awareness** – you feel like you *are* the activity; there's no separation between yourself and the task.
- **Clear goals** – you have a clear sense of what you're trying to achieve, and the steps you need to take are well defined.
- **Loss of self-consciousness** – you're so involved that you're not worried about how you're perceived or what others might think.
- **Timelessness** – time seems to distort; hours can pass by in what feels like minutes.
- **Autotelic experience** – the activity is intrinsically rewarding, you're doing it for its own sake, not for any external reward.

When was the last time you were in a state of flow? No doubt it was when you were doing something you enjoyed. I believe it is the same for students. When learning feels meaningful, manageable and motivating, students are far more likely to enter that focused, energised state where time seems to disappear and learning feels natural. Our challenge is to help them get there!

Factors affecting attention in the classroom

Multitasking

When it comes to paying attention, multitasking is a myth. While many people believe they can handle several tasks at once, research consistently shows that what's actually happening is rapid task-switching, not simultaneous processing. The human brain can only focus on one complex task at a time. When attempting to multitask, it divides attention between tasks, switching back and forth rapidly. This reduces the quality of focus and performance on each task.

When students are asked to shift their focus from one activity, subject or type of task to another, there's a temporary decline in performance or attention as their brain adjusts to the new task. Although it is only temporary, for some students, time spent on learning can be considerably decreased as they try and regain their focus.

Here's how it plays out in the classroom:

- **Loss of focus.** If students are constantly shifting between different activities or subjects in a short time span, it disrupts their focus and reduces the quality of their attention. For example, if a lesson involves frequent transitions between group work, individual tasks and class discussions, students are likely to find it hard to concentrate or follow along as they have to continuously adjust to new demands.

- **Time to reorient.** Every time a student switches tasks, there's often a 'reorientation' phase. During this time, students might be distracted or slow to regain focus. In classrooms where transitions happen frequently, the cumulative effect of these switches can result in decreased overall attention throughout the lesson.

- **Task complexity.** The more complex or unfamiliar a new task is, the higher the cognitive 'cost' of switching. For example, a student who moves from a familiar maths lesson to a highly abstract or unfamiliar subject may struggle to focus and engage immediately. Structured transitions, such as short breaks or warm-up activities, can help ease this switch and re-prime the brain for learning.

- **Implication for classroom management.** Teachers should keep in mind that switching between tasks or activities can be mentally tiring for students. If there are too many transitions, or if they happen too quickly, students may find it harder to stay focused and engaged. To help with this, it's a good idea to plan for smooth transitions by grouping similar activities together and giving students a bit of time to reset when moving from one subject to another.

Students' attention span usually increases with age, however, Table 1 is a reminder that sometimes our expectations as teachers do not match the students' developmental stage. It shows the approximate ranges for *focused, sustained attention* on a single task. Children can often re-engage for far longer when they are highly motivated or when tasks are broken into varied, manageable chunks.

Table 1: Student attention spans

Age of student	Typical concentration span	Notes
4 years	8–12 minutes	Can focus for slightly longer, especially with visual or engaging materials
5 years	10–15 minutes	Ready for short group tasks or guided learning activities
6–7 years	12–18 minutes	Can handle more structured tasks; scaffolding still useful
8–9 years	16–24 minutes	Can sustain focus on moderately challenging tasks
10–12 years	20–30 minutes	Capable of longer, independent work with appropriate support

Sources: Center on the Developing Child at Harvard University (2016); Simon et al. (2023)

Distractors

These come in all shapes and sizes. However, there are two main types: sensory and emotional. The sensory issues are more straightforward to address and, as a result, they tend to be resolved more quickly. Emotional distractions, on the other hand, are a greater challenge. Much will

depend on an individual's ability to stop the 'loop of worry', or the 'loop of excitement', by reframing their situation using the executive function cognitive flexibility, AKA, Thinking flexibly in the SOWATT framework. When students' minds wander, their brains activate a host of brain circuits that 'chatter' about things that have nothing to do with what they were trying to learn. This lack of focus means they will be unable to store any memories of what they were learning. The power to disengage our attention from one thing and move it to another is, therefore, essential not only for learning, but for our wellbeing.

What it might look like in a classroom

In a Year 4 classroom, students are engaged in an inquiry lesson about sustainability. The teacher has just introduced a group task: "Explore how plastic waste affects ocean life using books, printed articles and tablet research, then present the findings on a poster".

At first, the class appears busy, but focus quickly drifts. In one group, Zoe flips through a book without reading, distracted by a conversation at the next table. Mason opens a website but soon begins clicking random links, ending up on an unrelated page. In another group, Ava keeps switching between writing headings and colouring the poster title, never fully settling on one task.

Several students move between materials without completing any part of the activity, frequently asking what they were supposed to be doing or waiting for someone else to take the lead. Noise gradually increases as conversations stray off-topic, and the teacher has to pause to redirect multiple groups, with little sustained attention being given to the actual research or planning. Does this sound familiar?

SOWATT can teachers do?

Mindset and Motivation

(Why paying attention matters and keeping students engaged)

- **Explain to students why the skill of attention is important.**

- **Incorporate some element of choice and autonomy.** Students sustain attention better when doing something they enjoy.
- **Make liberal use of specific praise.**
- **Find the fun!**

Environmental and Structural Supports

(Setting up the classroom and routines to optimise focus)

- **Check the temperature and air quality**; open windows if needed.
- **Know the students as individuals** so teachers can pick up on changes in a student's mood and follow up as required.
- **Establish clear expectations and routines:**
    - *Set clear objectives.* When students know what the lesson is about and what's expected of them, they are more likely to stay engaged.
    - *Use a routine.* Having consistent lesson structures can help students mentally prepare for transitions and focus on the content.
    - *Give clear instructions.* Provide short, clear instructions and check for understanding before proceeding.
- **Decrease clutter and visual distractions.** This is particularly important for students who have difficulty focusing.
- **Use a method of random selection when checking for understanding.** This requires all students to focus on the lesson, as their name is likely to be randomly selected from pop sticks to answer a question.
- **Use a visual timer** (for example, Time Timer) to indicate elapsed time.
- **Keep moving around the room** to give prompts/encouragement.
- **Use random selection** to keep all students attentive.
- **Design lessons that encourage flow** by finding the right balance between challenge and skill for students to avoid them looking for distractions when they are having difficulties.

Teaching and Learning Strategies

(Explicit strategies to develop attention, focus and self-regulation)

- **Explicitly teach students *how* to pay attention.** It cannot be assumed that they know! What does it look like in practice?
- **Start lessons with a thought-provoking or open-ended question** to spark curiosity.
- **Provide time for targeted practice and get students to monitor themselves using a tally chart.** Reflect on what they discover. Can they identify what distracts them? How might they improve their ability to sustain attention?
- **Use call-and-response cues to orient students to learning.** It will look different in different classrooms, however, here are some examples to get you started:
    - "Macaroni and cheese"... "Everyone freeze"
    - "Hocus pocus"... "Everybody focus!"
    - "One, two, three, eyes on me"... "One, two, eyes on you!"
    - "Hands on top"... "Everybody stop!" (while putting both hands on head)
    - "And a hush fell across the room!"... "Hushhhhh!"
    - "Waterfall"... "Shhhhhh"
    - "Flat tyre"... "Shhhh"
    - "All set?"... "You bet!"
    - "Good, better"... "Best!"... "Never let it"... "Rest!" "Until your good is"... "Better!"... "And your better is the"... "Best!"
- **Introduce short mindfulness activities** (breathing, attention to the present).
- **Teach responsively.** Regularly check for understanding using five main techniques (Sherrington & Caviglioli, 2022):
    - Summarising
    - Repeating instructions
    - Agree or disagree
    - Make a plan and talk it through
    - Explain or defend your position

- **Develop the skill of 'comparing'**, where students are required to notice/discuss the similarities between things. In lower primary this might be at a more concrete level, for example, comparing photos of their town 50 years ago with photos of what it looks like today. Older students will be able to compare two texts or even two ideas.
- **Introduce some short mindfulness activities** to encourage students to pay attention to their breathing and how they can control this.
- **Incorporate movement/sound effects into stories.** Assign different characters a specific movement or sound. As the story unfolds, students listen for the character's name and makes the appropriate response.

SOWATT can students do?

- Practise being in control of their attention!
- Look at people when they are talking to them and practise active listening – actively engage.
- Plan ahead to avoid creating distractions for them and their peers, for example, go to the bathroom in recess, ensure electrical devices are charged before the lesson.
- Minimise distractions on their table.
- Sit in an optimal position in the class – not sitting next to a peer who they know is not a good fit for them and learning. Ask themselves questions such as:
    - "Will this spot help me avoid distractions?"
    - "Can I see and hear the teacher clearly from here?"
    - "Am I sitting near people who help me stay on task or distract me?"
    - "Do I feel comfortable and ready to learn in this space?"
- Be prepared at the start of the lesson (toileted, not hungry, equipment ready).
- Engage actively with the teacher – ask questions, volunteer to answer questions and respond to prompts.
- Use active listening strategies – focus on main ideas, make connections to previous learning.

- Set a timer, for example, read for 10 minutes. Start small and build up. A good analogy is building stamina like an athlete. The Pomodoro Technique can be used (i.e. setting a timer for a designated time – age dependant – and then taking a five-minute break).
- Listen to feedback – they might not get accurate feedback from the voice inside their head.
- Check in with themselves – "Am I still focused?" If not, pause and refocus.
- Reflect at the end of lessons – "What helped me focus today?" "What got in the way?"
- Do some physical activity each day.

SOWATT can parents do?

- Limit the amount of screentime and do not let children use screens in the bedroom.
- Ensure children get sufficient sleep each night.
- Build focus through play, for example, puzzles, boardgames – play them *together*.
- Refrain from trying to have conversations across rooms – it's better to be in the same room so you are face to face.
- Create a clutter-free study area – remove distractions when students are doing homework; this includes closing doors so they are not distracted by what other members of the family are doing.
- Praise effort and celebrate small wins.
- Model sustained attention.

> **Joke:**
>
> "My partner says that I am not good at listening or paying attention to them. At least that's what I think they said."

My summary

What are your key takeaways?

How does this chapter relate to what you already know or do?

Chapter 7

Thinking flexibly

"Many of the truths that we cling to depend on our point of view"
— Obi-Wan Kenobi (*Star Wars: Return of the Jedi*)

Thinking flexibly refers to:

- Shifting mindsets
- Considering other people's views (empathy)
- Coping with change
- Generating different solutions to problems
- Switching from big picture to details (important for reading)

Why is it important?

Cognitive flexibility, or thinking flexibly, is incredibly important for students because it equips them with the ability to adapt their thinking, adjust strategies and handle new and unexpected situations. In today's fast-changing world, these skills are essential not just for academic success, but for navigating life in general – being able to shift your perspective on a situation can do wonders for your wellbeing.

In the classroom, students are often exposed to complex concepts that may challenge their initial understanding. The ability to think flexibly helps them process new information more effectively and integrate it with what they already know.

It also allows students to consider multiple solutions to a problem. This is essential for critical thinking, as it encourages them to evaluate a range of options rather than fixating on a single solution. For example, in maths or science, a flexible thinker can approach a problem from different angles and find the most effective strategy. Working together with metacognition, it also helps students recognise when a particular approach isn't working, requiring them to pivot and try a new strategy without getting stuck in a rigid mindset.

The ability to think flexibly is important when working with others, particularly in group settings. Students often need to adjust their ideas based on the input of others, resolve conflicts and be willing to change their perspective. This entails them to think flexibly by considering other people's viewpoints and integrating them into the group's process.

Furthermore, cognitive flexibility is linked to emotional intelligence. It enables students to recognise that their initial emotional reactions to a situation can change, and that they can alter their perspective to respond more effectively. It allows them to reframe the situation, see it as a learning opportunity and adjust their approach accordingly. This is especially important for handling stress, frustration or failure, all of which are part of the learning process.

What it might look like in the classroom

In a Year 3 classroom, a relief teacher is covering for the day while the regular teacher is away. The students have just returned from recess, and the teacher announces a change to the usual routine: instead of their usual science project, they will be doing a creative writing task based on a short video clip.

As soon as the change is mentioned, several students become visibly unsettled. Emily frowns and repeatedly asks when they will be doing science, insisting that it is 'science day'. Lucas refuses to take out his writing book, sitting with his arms crossed and saying, "This isn't what

we're supposed to do." A few others flip through their planners, trying to prove that the schedule is wrong.

When the video starts, some students are still preoccupied with the change, whispering to each other about the missing science project. During the writing task, several struggle to shift their focus to the new topic. One student keeps trying to relate the writing back to their science project from last week, while another becomes frustrated and asks to go to the sick bay.

The teacher tries to move the lesson forward, but the class remains distracted, unsettled by the change in routine and unable to adapt to the shift in expectations.

SOWATT can teachers do?

Mindset and Motivation

(Helping students see the value of flexible thinking and promoting curiosity)

- **Explain what cognitive flexibility is** and why it is important.
- **Provide feedback** so that students are aware of when they are using flexible thinking.
- **Promote a growth mindset** by emphasising effort and strategies over innate ability and focusing on the learning process rather than just the end product.
- **Help students reframe negative experiences.** Reframing situations can help build resilience and avoid catastrophising when life doesn't go as expected.
- **Find the fun!**

Environmental and Structural Supports

(Creating a classroom environment that encourages flexible thinking)

- **Create a safe, supportive classroom culture.** We can't expect students to flex their thinking if there is a fear of 'being wrong'. It is

vital that students feel comfortable to share their ideas, collaborate and learn from others.
- **Be intentional in planning, implementing and evaluating** activities that promote cognitive flexibility.
- **Use restorative justice scripts in conflict resolution,** requiring consideration of alternative perspectives.

Teaching and Learning Strategies

(Explicit instructional strategies to develop flexible thinking)

- **Ask open-ended questions.**
- **Use a question matrix** to encourage different ways of asking questions (see an example on page 171).
- **Provide opportunities for open-ended tasks** – particularly ones that may generate more than one correct answer. Or number stories at the beginning of a maths lesson which may be solved in different ways.
- **Promote opportunities to problem solve.** Presenting problems that require creative thinking and multiple steps to solve, either in a group or individually, requires students to negotiate, adapt and refine their ideas.
- **Promote curiosity** by encouraging multiple viewpoints and solutions. For instance, when discussing a topic, ask questions like, "What are some other ways we might approach this?" This includes exposing students to new ideas and offering them opportunities to engage with new concepts, methods and information that challenge their existing knowledge.
- **Have structured discussions, which require students to think critically**, defend their positions and be open to reconsidering their views based on evidence. Structured debates are especially powerful in developing cognitive flexibility because they push students to think from multiple perspectives.
- **Play 'What if...' or 'Would you rather...'** Introducing hypothetical scenarios challenges students to think flexibly by imagining how they would respond to different situations. It encourages them to consider

different possible outcomes and reframe their thinking when new information arises.

- **Teach students how to create concept maps.** These help students visualise how different ideas or concepts connect. They're a powerful tool for promoting cognitive flexibility because students have to adjust their thinking as they make connections between different pieces of information.
- **Change the rules to familiar games.**
- **Write alternative endings to favourite stories.**
- **Explore oxymorons.** Challenge students to use them in their writing, for example, bittersweet, deafening silence, only choice, original copy, minor crisis, virtual reality!
- **Have fun telling jokes.** Many jokes and familiar expressions rely on double entendres. Have fun finding and using them, for example, "fork in the road", "you need to pull your socks up".
- **Model flexible thinking and perspective-taking.** There's no point teaching the skill if you don't model it yourself! Be aware of your reactions when there is a change to your schedule or you've forgotten your lunch – reframing your thinking aloud is a powerful tool and shows students that the ability to be flexible in our thinking is necessary at all ages. Playing the 'Devil's advocate' once in a while will also force students to shift their thinking – to defend their viewpoint if nothing else!
- **Teach The Catastrophe Scale.** It's great for putting things into perspective.

SOWATT can students do?

- Practise perspective-taking. Students can practise this by intentionally trying to understand other people's perspectives, whether in class discussions, debates or group projects by asking themselves: "What might someone else with a different opinion or background think about this?"

- Engage in regular problem solving. Engaging with complex or unfamiliar problems forces students to adapt their thinking, so regularly playing strategy games including sudoku, crosswords and chess, should be encouraged.
- Be open to new challenges. This doesn't come easy to some students, particularly those with perfectionist tendencies and fixed mindsets.
- Seek feedback and adapt. Seeking feedback from teachers, peers or mentors helps students identify areas of improvement and adjust their approach.
- Embrace mistakes and learn from them. Viewing mistakes as learning opportunities is key to developing cognitive flexibility.
- Ask open-ended questions. Questions to be encouraged to provoke deeper thinking and flexibility include:
  - "What if the opposite were true?"
  - "How would someone from a different culture think about this?"
  - "What would happen if we took this idea in a different direction?"
- Teach students to practise *positive self-talk* to challenge negative or unhelpful thoughts. *Reframing* a situation can help regulate emotional responses. For example, instead of thinking, "I can't do this," they could reframe it as, "This is tough, but I can handle it step by step."

SOWATT can parents do?

- Encourage open-mindedness, by playing 'the devil's advocate'.
- Model cognitive flexibility. Show your child how to approach problems with a flexible mindset by demonstrating it in your daily life. If you encounter a challenge or setback, narrate your thought process out loud, explaining how you adjust your approach and stay open to different solutions.
- Encourage problem solving and decision-making. Present your child with problems (age appropriate) and involve them in thinking through different ways to solve the issue. Be sure to highlight that

there can be multiple solutions to a problem, and encourage them to evaluate the pros and cons of each.
- Provide opportunities for failure and resilience. How to do it: let your child experience challenges and failures, but frame these moments as learning experiences. Teach them that it's OK to change strategies when things don't work out and that failure is often the first step towards finding a better solution.
- Encourage creative play.
- Praise effort, not just results. Reinforcing effort and persistence teaches children that flexibility in thinking leads to growth, not just success.
- Problem solve things together.
- Encourage empathy by not being quick to judge others.
- Give a time warning if you know your child struggles with transitioning from one activity to another.
- Use dynamic learning activities that require strategic thinking, such as chess or role-playing games. These sorts of opportunities provide students with the potential to practise switching between different strategies and scenarios, based on evolving conditions.

Joke:

Q: Why can't you explain puns to kleptomaniacs?

A: They always take things literally.

My summary

What are your key takeaways?

How does this chapter relate to what you already know or do?

Chapter 8

Thinking about thinking

"The greatest teacher, failure is"

– Yoda (*Star Wars*)

Thinking about thinking refers to:

The ability to think about, regulate and monitor one's own thinking processes. It helps us learn from mistakes and supports students to be in control of their learning – it puts the SELF into self-regulation.

Metacognition, AKA 'thinking about thinking', literally means 'going beyond' or 'rising above' the learning process. The term was first coined by John Flavell (1979), to describe how learners adjust their approach to a task when the desired results are not being achieved. A reciprocal relationship exists between metacognition and learning (Ohtani & Hisasaka, 2018), that is, students who are able to consciously think about their thinking tend to be more independent and take greater responsibility for their own learning. Some students naturally develop metacognitive skills, while others may struggle to do so without being explicitly taught. Research (Ohtani & Hisasaka, 2018) shows that using metacognition significantly improves student progress, which is why it is essential that we focus on helping all learners acquire this vital skill. This involves creating classrooms where learners regularly analyse their own thinking and are open to adjusting their approach when necessary.

A major Education Endowment Foundation (EEF) meta-analysis found that teaching metacognition alongside self-regulation strategies can lead to an average of eight-plus months' additional progress in a school year, particularly for disadvantaged students (EEF, 2018). These benefits are strongest when strategies are taught in context, like planning before writing or evaluating during problem solving in maths.

Moreover, metacognitive practices are strongly linked to self-efficacy, which is a key predictor of motivation and wellbeing. Zimmerman (2000) found that self-regulated learners – those who actively apply metacognitive strategies – tend to have stronger beliefs in their ability to succeed, which boosts both performance and emotional wellbeing. Other studies show that teaching these strategies can lead to better learning *and* help students feel more capable and emotionally balanced (Dignath & Büttner, 2008).

The ability to monitor one's own learning and make conscious decisions about how to improve is essential for personal progress, whether in school, in a career or in life. It is metacognition that enables students to recognise when something isn't working, stop to consider alternative solutions and make adjustments to improve outcomes. This flexible, conscious approach to problem solving is key to success and mental wellbeing. When students are able to assess their progress, consider different strategies and make improvements based on reflection, they are more likely to achieve their goals and feel in control of their academic journey. Metacognition, therefore, is absolutely vital if students are to drive their own learning and approach new challenges with greater independence and resilience.

Metacognition is actually more nuanced than you might think. A common conception of metacognition is that there are two parts: *metacognitive knowledge* and *metacognitive regulation*.

Figure 7 (based on the EEF, 2018) visually explains the two key components of metacognition: metacognitive knowledge and metacognitive regulation, and how they work together in a continuous learning cycle.

Figure 7: The two key components of metacognition

Metacognitive knowledge – this is what the learner knows about learning. It is divided into three types:

- **Knowledge of task** – understanding what a task involves, including its purpose, demands or difficulty, for example, "This is a tricky word problem, I need to read it carefully."
- **Knowledge of strategies** – knowing different ways to approach learning or solve problems, for example, "I can use a number line to subtract."
- **Knowledge of self** – awareness of one's own abilities, strengths, preferences and limits, for example, "I learn better when I work with a partner."

These types of knowledge inform how students approach and reflect on their learning.

Metacognitive regulation – this refers to how the learner controls and manages their thinking during the learning process. It happens across three phases:

1. **Before** (planning) – setting goals, selecting strategies, predicting challenges. This could involve setting goals, selecting appropriate

strategies and determining what resources you will need. For instance, planning for a research project might involve deciding which sources to use, how to organise your time and which tools you'll need for data collection. Or it can be as simple as, "I will draw a picture before I start writing."

2. **During** (monitoring) – while students are working on a task, they need to keep track of their progress. Are they understanding the material? Is the strategy they're using effective? If a student is writing a story, monitoring might involve checking that the sequence of events is plausible, or whether they are staying on topic. It is an ongoing process of self-reflection, for example, "This isn't working – maybe I need to try something else."

3. **After** (evaluating) – after completing a task, students evaluate how well they did. This could mean reflecting on the outcome, assessing whether the strategies were effective and identifying what could be improved for next time. For example, after a test, evaluating might involve a student reviewing which questions they struggled with and thinking about how they could improve their preparation for next time, for example, "Next time I'll underline key words in the question before I start."

Students need to use both metacognitive knowledge (what they know about their learning) and metacognitive regulation (how they manage their learning) to become more independent, strategic, reflective and self-regulated learners.

What level of metacognition can you expect?

As a teacher, your aim is to develop all aspects of metacognition, although your expectations will vary depending on the age group of your class and their previous experience of the metacognitive process.

Research is telling us that metacognition begins to develop in the preschool years (Braund, 2022), hence there is a need to support and further develop these skills in the primary years and beyond. By the age of 5–7, children begin to show basic metacognitive skills, such as recognising when they don't understand something (Whitebread et al., 2009). Younger primary students (Years Foundation to 2) tend to use this knowledge situationally, often with prompts, whereas older primary students (Years 4–6) begin to use it deliberately and independently, transferring it across subjects. However, these skills are fragile and inconsistent unless they are explicitly taught and scaffolded by adults (Veenman et al., 2006). Just prompting students to 'think about their thinking' is not enough. Instruction must be explicit, sustained and embedded in real tasks (Zohar & Barzilai, 2013).

In the SOWATT approach, metacognition can be thought of as a bridge linking the five other elements so that they work together more effectively. When students think about their thinking, they are better placed to resist impulsive decisions (self-regulation), plan how to approach a task (organisation), stay focused on what matters (attention), hold and manage information as they work (working memory) and shift strategies when needed (thinking flexibly). Metacognition helps students step back, notice what's working or not and make adjustments. Without it, these skills can feel disconnected. However, with it, students are better able to take control of their learning and become more independent and reflective learners.

What this might look like in a classroom

In a Year 5 classroom, the students had just finished a tricky maths task on problem-solving strategies. Their teacher asked them to take a moment and think about how they tackled the problems and the strategies they used.

As the students looked over their work, one of them noticed she had used the same method for every question, even though some problems could have been solved more easily with a different approach. She realised she had done it out of habit and thought about how she could mix things up next time by considering which strategy would work best for each problem.

Another student looked at his incorrect answers and realised he hadn't taken the time to really read the questions before jumping in. He thought about how he could get better by first taking a moment to carefully think through the problem and understand what was being asked before starting to solve it.

At another desk, a group of students thought about how they worked together on their group task. They realised that even though they finished quickly, some people had done more of the work, and they hadn't really talked through their solutions. They decided they could work better next time by making sure everyone was involved in solving each step and discussing the answers together.

By the end of the reflection time, the students had a mix of insights. Some were really good at recognising how they were thinking and what they could improve, while others were just starting to understand how they could change the way they approached problems.

SOWATT can teachers do?

There are three key questions that are vital for teachers to ask when developing metacognition because they address core aspects of how metacognitive skills evolve and how students can be empowered to think about their thinking (Keable, 2025).

1. **How can I support students' belief in their own ability to learn?**
   - Metacognitive processes require students to have confidence in their own abilities to manage their learning. If students do not believe they can improve or succeed, they are less likely to engage in reflective thinking or take on challenging tasks. This self-belief forms the foundation for their metacognitive development.
   - This question also addresses students' self-efficacy, which is a key part of their metacognitive knowledge. When students understand that their efforts can lead to growth, they are more likely to develop a good sense of what they know and what strategies work for them in various learning contexts.
   - Belief in their ability to learn encourages students to regulate their own learning more effectively. They are more likely to engage in self-monitoring, adjusting strategies and persisting in the face of difficulty if they believe their actions can lead to improvement.

2. **How can I promote familiarity with the learning process?**
   - To think about their thinking, students need to first be aware of how learning works. If students understand how learning

happens – what steps, strategies and methods lead to success – they can begin to manage their own learning and monitor their progress.

- Familiarity with the learning process helps students build metacognitive knowledge, which includes awareness of different learning strategies, the nature of tasks, and their own strengths and weaknesses. This knowledge is essential for making informed decisions about how to approach problems or assignments.
- Understanding the learning process also supports regulation. When students know how to break tasks down, set goals and monitor their progress, they can better control how they learn, choosing the right strategies and adjusting them as necessary.

3. **How can I ensure that students are capable of independent thought?**
    - Metacognition thrives when students can think independently and reflect on their own thinking without constant external input. Developing independent thought is crucial for helping students become lifelong learners, who are able to navigate challenges and solve problems without being overly reliant on others.
    - Independent thought requires students to be aware of the strategies that work best for them and to recognise when they need to adjust their approach. Metacognitive knowledge helps them identify their cognitive processes, strengths and weaknesses, giving them the tools to work independently.
    - Independent thought also involves self-regulation – students must be able to monitor their understanding, adjust their approaches and apply strategies autonomously. As they develop metacognitive regulation skills, they are able to independently guide their learning and overcome obstacles more effectively.

When teachers address these three questions, they are not just teaching content; they are laying the groundwork for students to understand their own cognitive processes, regulate their learning and gain the confidence to tackle challenges independently. These questions push students to understand the 'what' and 'how' of their learning: what strategies are effective, what processes they use and what steps they need to take to succeed. They help students develop the ability to monitor and control their thinking. If students believe they can learn and understand the learning process, they are more likely to engage in active regulation, adjusting their strategies, evaluating their progress and modifying their approach as needed. These questions also highlight the importance of experience. The more students are encouraged to reflect on their learning and apply strategies independently, the more they develop metacognitive experience. This hands-on practice with thinking about thinking helps them refine their skills over time.

As teachers, our attitude towards students and their learning is so important. Unfortunately, some students will have unconsciously formed a poor view of themselves as learners even before they have stepped into a primary school. Teachers need to demonstrate an unwavering belief in a student's ability to achieve whatever we're expecting of them and, when necessary, show endless patience as we strive to override their previous views of what's possible. We have to place a 'value' on every student, ensuring absolutely no putdowns are allowed in our classroom, not even a student saying something negative about themselves. The development of a growth mindset, as described on page 37, is crucial to support students' self-efficacy.

What we praise also has a bearing on how much responsibility a student feels able to take on in relation to their own learning. If we reward completed work, neatly presented work, compliance with the instructional template, always answering correctly, remaining quiet, not asking for help, etc., then we're killing off any potential for metacognitive thought. There's also no guarantee with any of the above that 'learning' has actually taken place. We therefore need to be promoting the learning process: praising focus, effort and persistence so that students realise their role is not to please the teacher, but to take responsibility for their own progress.

In addition to fostering a growth mindset and providing specific, actionable feedback to students, teachers need to create *communities of learners* (Slavin, 2020). In the context of primary schools, it emphasises collaboration, mutual respect and active engagement in the learning process. Research has consistently shown that collaborative learning leads to better problem-solving skills, higher engagement and greater retention of knowledge. A study by Slavin (2020) found that cooperative learning strategies in primary schools positively impact both academic performance and social-emotional development.

SOWATT else can teachers do?

Mindset and Motivation

(Helping students value metacognition and develop a reflective, growth-oriented approach)

- **Explain what metacognition is** and why it is important – before, during and after learning.
- **Provide timely, process-focused feedback** to develop students' **self-awareness** – being able to recognise *what I'm doing, how I'm feeling, and how my actions affect my learning and others.* When we acknowledge a student's effort ("You kept trying even when it was hard!"), dopamine signals the brain: *That felt good, I'll do it again!*
- **Celebrate success and effort** – acknowledge when students use metacognitive strategies effectively.
- **Monitor emotional responses to learning** – help students recognise frustration, confusion or confidence and re-engage appropriately.
- **Find the fun!**

Environmental and Structural Supports

(Classroom routines, tools and systems to scaffold metacognition)

- **Create routines** that include planning (before), monitoring (during) and evaluating (after) tasks.
- **Use charts or daily tracking** systems for effort, productivity and collaboration skills.
- **Use coloured blocks** (red, yellow, green) to indicate confidence levels for tasks. As students start their independent work, they select a coloured block to denote how confident they feel about how to proceed: red = completely stuck; yellow = I will give it a go, but not confident; green = confident. This not only forces students to reflect

on their level of confidence but also provides excellent feedback to the teacher as to where the immediate needs are within the classroom.
- **Provide opportunities for collaboration** – metacognition is not necessarily an individual activity and may be developed by social interactions that prompt students to externalise their thinking, reflect on others' strategies and promote deeper reflection. It's the idea that students can build off each other's ideas and be responsive to peer feedback. Think-Pair-Share is a useful strategy to clarify understanding. First, reflect on questions or ideas independently, then share with a partner. This encourages students to process their thinking before discussing it.

Teaching and Learning Strategies

(Explicit instruction and practice to develop metacognitive skills)

- **Model metacognition.** Teachers can model how they approach problems, break tasks into manageable steps and review their thinking process aloud, including the use of *prompting questions*. For example, when solving a maths problem, you might say, "First, I need to understand the question. Now, I'll think about what I already know about this topic. What strategy should I use? I think I'll try…" By vocalising your thinking, you show students how to plan, monitor and evaluate their own cognitive processes.
- **Teach the language** of metacognition, such as 'strategy', 'plan', 'reflect', 'evaluate', 'monitor' and 'adjust'. Regularly use this language in class to help students build familiarity and reinforce the practice of thinking about their thinking.
- **Use metacognitive prompts and questions.** See the resources section on page 155 for examples, and for an example of their use to support students' persuasive writing.
- **Model problem-solving dialogue.** Use language like, "Let's stop and think for a moment. What's another way to solve this?" or "How do you know you understood this correctly?" Articulate how you solve problems – whether it is a maths problem, writing task or science experiment, demonstrate how to approach a problem step by step.

As you work through it, narrate what you are thinking and how you adjust your approach if something isn't working.

- **Teach the 'Think, Plan, Do, Review' cycle.** This can be particularly helpful when working on longer, creative tasks:
  - *Think:* Encourage students to think about the task before they start. For example, "What do I already know about this?" or "What do I need to find out?"
  - *Plan:* Guide students in making a plan before they dive into the task. For example, "How will I approach this?" or "What materials or strategies will I need?"
  - *Do:* Allow them to carry out their plan. Encourage them to be mindful of the strategies they're using as they work.
  - *Review:* After completing the task, have students reflect on how things went. For example, "What worked well?" and "What could I do differently next time?"

  This review process helps students recognise the effectiveness of their strategies.

- **Promote self-awareness** through reflection on effort, focus and collaboration – see sample rubrics in the resources section on page 161.
- **Teach self-questioning strategies**, for example, using the WIT strategy. Encourage students to ask themselves questions during the learning process:
  - **W**hat am I trying to do?
  - **I**s it working?
  - **T**ry something different if I get stuck.
- **Use questions to promote metacognition throughout the learning process:**
  - **Before a task**
    - Why am I doing this task?
    - Why is it helpful to think ahead?
    - Why might I need more than one strategy?
  - **During a task**
    - Why am I finding this confusing?

- ○ Why should I keep going even if it's hard?
- ○ Why do I need to pause and think here?
- **After a task**
  - ○ Why did my approach work (or not work)?
  - ○ Why did I succeed or struggle with this task?
  - ○ Why would I do it differently next time?

- Consider introducing **reflective journals** in the upper primary years. Students are encouraged to reflect upon and evaluate their learning process, their strengths and areas to improve upon. Questions like, "What worked well for you today?" and "What would you do differently next time?" can guide them to reflect on their learning. Remember to vary the prompts to maintain motivation. For building greater self-awareness, students can record work productivity or effort on a daily chart, or graph and track their progress over time. Such charts are often negatively associated with students on 'behaviour management plans', however, putting a positive spin on it allows everyone to be more aware of their effort, time management and collaboration skills. You can customise the charts for the needs of your class, but some suggestions are: class participation, ability to get along with others, ability to initiate tasks or stay on track. Highlighting important study skills in this way brings them to a conscious level and helps to build good learning habits.

- **Teach the 'Fist of Five'** - this can be used in a variety of ways, for example, at the end of a lesson or activity. By asking, "How confident do you feel about…?", students are required to reflect on what they learned and how well they understood it.
  - 5 fingers = I fully understand and could explain it to someone else
  - 4 fingers = I understand it but might need a little help
  - 3 fingers = I'm getting there but still have questions
  - 2 fingers = I don't understand much and need help
  - 1 finger (or a closed fist) = I'm completely confused

  Used regularly, this strategy becomes a scaffold for students to monitor, evaluate and plan their own learning. It also gives them a voice in the learning process, encouraging them to take responsibility for seeking help when needed.

- **Co-construct** understanding with students using open-ended questions and think-alouds, for example, "How do we know if this answer is correct? What evidence do we have?"
- Provide regular, specific feedback (for example, the WISE structure – see Chapter 2).

SOWATT can students do?

- Develop awareness of their personal strengths and weaknesses.
- Develop a willingness to engage in and improve their own learning.
- Practise monitoring progress and asking for help when appropriate.
- Practise talking about how they have done something, or what they have learned.
- Develop awareness of the strategies they have used to complete tasks and why they were helpful.
- Make goals and be aware of the steps involved in achieving them, including tracking progress.

SOWATT can parents do?

- Share their thinking and how they got to a particular viewpoint.
- Ask open-ended questions to prompt reflection.
- Be very careful about what they say 'to' and 'about' their child, remembering that they may be overheard.
- Never use negative self-talk yourself; rather, model sharing out loud a positive view of your own abilities.
- Always verbalise a positive view of school and demonstrate your belief in a child's ability as a learner.
- Don't accept perceived 'limitations' and provide plenty of opportunities for a learner to develop the skills needed to overcome them.
- Help them to appreciate the purpose of their comfort zone and the need to leave it in order to learn.

- Model a 'can do' attitude towards 'challenge' and demonstrate excitement at the opportunity to learn from it.
- View mistakes as an essential part of the process, explaining that the brain learns and adapts from those more memorable experiences.
- Emphasise the importance of 'practise' to make learning stick.
- Give children the opportunity to shoulder some practical responsibility at home before relating that to doing the same with their learning.
- Allow children to see you 'change your mind' sometimes and always explain how new information has led you to have a different view.
- The subconscious brain believes everything it's told, so help your children remove the word 'can't' from their vocabulary.
- Help children see that the vital ingredient to success is the level of effort someone is prepared to put in, not a predestined ability.

> **Joke:**
> "I've started telling everyone about the benefits of eating dried grapes. It's all about raisin' awareness."

My summary

What are your key takeaways?

How does this chapter relate to what you already know or do?

Chapter 9

Unpacking the curriculum through the SOWATT lens

"In nature everything is connected, interwoven, subject to natural law. We cannot separate ourselves from that, no matter how hard we try"

– Jeffrey R. Anderson

Students cannot develop their cognition in isolation; rather, they need to develop these skills as they acquire subject knowledge (Willingham, 2007). Ideally, all staff at a school will have an understanding of the conditions required for executive functions to thrive and be able to view the various subjects that make up a primary curriculum through the SOWATT lens. The reason why this is optimal is because we only get better at something with practice. The more opportunities for practice, the greater the transfer across subjects, and the increased likelihood of information becoming automatised and stored in the long-term memory, which as you are aware, reduces the load on the working memory.

In this chapter, subjects are presented through the SOWATT lens. The examples are not exhaustive; indeed, you may see further ways in which a particular SOWATT skill could be used. The purpose of the following examples is to help you identify executive functions at work – being able to identify them in action is the first step towards planning for and scaffolding them.

Maths

Top five reasons students loose points in maths tests	
1. Not following instructions	
2. Sloppy writing/ presentation	
3. Confused by maths vocabulary	
4. Making errors on basic maths facts	
5. Not finishing – poor time management	

How can these issues be addressed?

Students need to...	What YOU can do
- Get emotions under control - Resist temptation to rush in - Persist	- *Encourage positive self-talk* - *Ask, "Have you got all the information you need?"* - *Offer positive encouragement*
- Answer questions in logical order – sequencing is important - Set work out neatly and orderly - Show the steps in thinking	- *Teach how to present work in a neat, orderly fashion* - *Model 'think-alouds'*
- Hold information in their head long enough to use it - Follow multi-step instructions - Break down the questions into manageable steps	- *Explain working memory to the student – it is limited and therefore we need to help it* - *Automatise basic questions*
- Read the question carefully - Work out what they are being asked to do	- *Teach how to identify key words*
- Know the vocabulary for different operations - Know that there can be different ways of getting an answer	- *Teach vocabulary: add, plus, sum of, addition, total, count on, tally* - *Teach and model different ways to get the answer – start the lesson with 'Number Talks'*
- Relate new problems to past experiences - Know which strategies to use and WHY - Monitor progress - Check answers	- *Ask, "When have you done something like this before?" or "What do you think you need to do and what makes you say that?"* - *Reflect – explain their thinking*

Reading

When we think about reading, we often focus on decoding words and understanding meaning. But there is much more going on in the brain than just recognising letters or following a storyline. Being a proficient reader is more than reading a book from start to finish; it involves all the SOWATT skills working together seamlessly.

	The key to focused reading is regulating your emotional reactions to what you're reading. For example, if you are reading a difficult section of a text, self-regulation helps you persist rather than give up or let frustration take over. It also involves pacing yourself – knowing when to slow down to understand complex ideas and when to speed up through more straightforward material. Without **self-regulation**, it's easy to lose track of the story or fail to understand a key concept, especially in long or complex texts. A reader who struggles with self-regulation might also skip over difficult parts without attempting to comprehend them, leading to gaps in understanding.
	**Organisation** is crucial because reading often requires us to track multiple ideas, characters or pieces of information simultaneously. For example, when reading a novel, keeping track of different plot lines or remembering details about each character's backstory requires a high level of mental organisation. Similarly, academic reading often requires understanding how different concepts fit together in a larger framework. A well-organised mind can more effectively remember, summarise and integrate information, which is key for both comprehension and retention. Without this skill, readers might get lost in the details, forget key information or fail to make connections between ideas.

When you're reading, you are constantly storing and updating bits of information as you progress. For example, you might need to remember the main idea of the first paragraph while you move on to the next one, or keep track of who said what in a conversation in a novel.

A strong **working memory** allows you to retain the information you've read so far and relate it to new information you come across later. Without it, comprehension suffers because you can't keep all the necessary details in mind long enough to connect them or build on previous ideas. You might end up rereading passages or losing track of the narrative thread, making reading less efficient.

Distractions – whether internal, like daydreaming, or external, like noise or other people – can easily disrupt reading. If your **attention** is divided, your comprehension and retention will likely suffer. Proficient readers are able to sustain their focus long enough to absorb and process what they're reading, filtering out irrelevant information or distractions.

When reading, **cognitive flexibility** allows you to adjust your understanding as new ideas or plot twists emerge. For example, a change in perspective or an unexpected piece of information might require you to reconsider your interpretation of a text. Readers who lack cognitive flexibility may struggle with texts that present contradictions, complex arguments or differing viewpoints.

Being able to shift gears mentally while reading – whether moving between different genres, adjusting to a different writing style or interpreting new ideas – is a hallmark of proficient reading. Without cognitive flexibility, readers may have difficulty processing new or challenging content, which can limit both their enjoyment and understanding of what they read.

When it comes to reading, this means reflecting on how well you're understanding the material, recognising when you're confused and taking steps to correct your comprehension. For instance, metacognitive readers might ask themselves, "What is the author trying to convey here?" or "Do I understand the key argument, or do I need to go back and review?"

Proficient readers are able to monitor their comprehension in real time, adjusting their strategies as needed. They might reread sections, look up unfamiliar words or take notes to solidify their understanding. Without **metacognitive skills**, a reader might not notice when they've missed key information or misunderstood a passage, leading to incomplete or faulty understanding.

Individually, these skills help readers process and understand texts. Together, they form a network of cognitive abilities that make reading both efficient and effective. In fact, many of these skills are interdependent; for instance, self-regulation supports sustained attention, and working memory aids in organising information.

Additionally, these cognitive skills don't just support comprehension of what we read in the moment – they also play a significant role in memory retention. A reader who can regulate their focus, flexibly adjust their thinking and monitor their own comprehension is more likely to retain and apply what they've read long after finishing the book or article.

Writing

For many students, being asked to write a story or a report and being presented with a blank piece of paper can be daunting. Indeed, you might well have been one of those students. There are many reasons for this, including attention difficulties, aversion, dysgraphia or executive function deficits.

Looking at the writing process through an executive function lens highlights the complexities of what is required when we write and provides a better understanding of not only why it can be a challenge, but also how we can better support the process.

The table opposite summarises the main stages in the writing process, the important role that executive functions play and some strategies/scaffolds that can be used to support each stage.

The writing process	Executive functions
Preview the writing prompt and determine the task, audience and purpose • Highlight key words • Provide thinking time • Get task clarity before proceeding • Provide a rubric and unpack the task	controlling emotions, not panicking reading the prompt carefully and identifying key words considering the audience, what would interest them, what they need to know asking, "When have I done something like this before?" and "What worked well previously?"
Planning • Use graphic organisers/mind map to help organise thoughts • Use different-coloured pens for different parts • Make time for this stage • Give credit for this stage • Provide checklists • Provide a timeline for completion	controlling the urge to get started and actually plan what is going to be written of thoughts, sequential thinking, prioritising, initiating the task keeping an idea in mind while considering others and sequencing them considering options monitoring the process
First draft • Some children may need a scribe or dictating software to help them get their ideas on paper • Use a word-processing program to make the subsequent stages easier • Remove potential distractions from students' working space; only have the resources that are needed for the task • Model the monitoring process using 'think-alouds'	persisting even if it's difficult of ideas into coherent text; creating micro goals for different sections sequential thinking of content while also considering rules of grammar and spelling being able to sustain attention on the task and avoid distractions considering options monitoring the process

The writing process	Executive functions
Revising/editing • Teach the acronyms CUPS for editing (Capital letters, Understanding, Punctuation, Spelling) and ARMS for revising (Add, Remove, Move, Substitute) • Provide checklists • Have anchor charts visible in the room • Teach how to use a thesaurus	not giving in to the temptation to finish before editing working systematically to edit and revise checking the writing for grammar, spelling, structure, the storyline, the audience considering word choices, character development and plot development; asking for feedback monitoring the process
Final copy • Increase motivation by empowering students' flexibility over final presentation	persevering until the end meeting deadlines being able to sustain attention on the task and avoid distractions monitoring the process
Feedback • Make time for this • Encourage peer feedback, for example, three stars and a wish • Celebrate and share success	setting a personal writing goal based on feedback asking, "What did I do well?" and "What could I improve on next time?"

As you can see, executive function skills and writing go hand in hand. With so much to consider, it's no wonder that writing can be such a laborious skill to master! The steps of the writing process, including prewriting, need to be taught through direct instruction, modelling and independent practice. While we ultimately want students to write independently, the process needs to be scaffolded to allow the student to learn effectively. We can remove that scaffolding gradually, as the process becomes automated.

Handwriting

The past couple of decades have seen a gradual decline in the importance paid to handwriting. For many years, there have been comments in staffrooms along the lines of, "It doesn't matter anymore, final exams will all be online soon, and no one will care about handwriting."

The fact of the matter is that this just hasn't happened, and my recent invigilation of Year 10 and 11 exams was proof that poor handwriting is, in fact, a handicap to learning. The number of students who were shaking weary wrists and flexing fingers midway through a two-hour exam was a sight to behold, especially to a primary school teacher who has spent countless hours honing her students' script into legible, well-formed masterpieces.

With a greater emphasis being put on the writing process, handwriting can be undervalued in many schools today. However, apart from being an important part of our identity (yes, we instantly know who has sent us a birthday card from the handwriting on the envelope), it needs to be valued from an executive function perspective.

	Once the basics have been mastered, handwriting becomes a perfect vehicle for **self-regulation**. The repetitive nature of joining letters and making patterns of letters has a soothing effect on a busy mind. It has a mindful quality, especially when paired with coloured pencils and some soothing background music – the precursor to the doodling we do as adults.
	Being ready to start! Have to hand: - a sharp pencil - a ruler - maybe even an eraser **Goal setting** can be very useful and motivating, particularly when the focus is on achieving one small aspect at a time, such as leaving the correct spacing between words.

	Handwriting requires holding and coordinating multiple pieces of information at once: remembering letter shapes, spelling and the sequence of strokes, while also planning and executing the motor movements. This coordination uses **working memory** to manage and integrate what the student is thinking and doing in real time.
	**Attention** is needed to focus on the basics before they are automatised: formation and orientation of letters; pencil grip and appropriate pressure; layout of page; and spacing of letters and words. Sustained attention is required to achieve this, especially for children who are just beginning to write.
	**Thinking flexibly** is called upon when changing across lower- and uppercases, especially when the letter bears no resemblance to each other, such as 'g' and 'G.'
	Continual monitoring of progress is required to avoid careless mistakes. It is also called upon to give ourselves a pat on the back when a student recognises the progress they are making.

Art

Art is typically seen as a medium for expression, a way to convey emotions and ideas. Emphasis tends to be placed on the end product rather than the process. When we unpack art through the SOWATT lens, it becomes obvious that it has so much more to offer than simply aesthetics. Engaging in both the creation and appreciation of art can significantly enhance executive functioning.

	**The art of managing emotions** Creating art allows children to express their feelings in a safe and constructive way. When they pick up a paintbrush or grab some markers, children learn to navigate their emotions – whether they're feeling joyful, frustrated or even a bit silly. This process helps them practise **self-regulation**. For example, when a child decides to turn a 'mistake' into part of their masterpiece, they're not just getting creative; they're also learning how to manage frustration and adapt to change.

Planning the masterpiece

Every great piece of art starts with a plan, and that's where **organisation** comes into play. Once children have gathered their materials, they should be encouraged to either sketch out their ideas, or at the very least articulate their ideas before diving in. This planning phase helps them understand the importance of organising their thoughts and resources. Whether they're sorting crayons or lining up paints, children will develop a knack for keeping things tidy – skills that will serve them well in school and beyond.

The art of remembering

Creating art often involves remembering specific details: the steps of a project, the colours they want to use or the techniques they've learned. This mental juggle strengthens **working memory**. For instance, while painting, a child might recall how to blend colours or the way they shaped clay last week. Each time they create, they're exercising their brain, building the capacity to hold and manipulate information in their minds.

Focus in the frame

Art requires a certain level of concentration. This focus enhances **attention** skills and encourages children to stay engaged with a task. Whether they're carefully painting a flower or intricately designing a collage, children learn to tune out distractions and commit to the moment.

The freedom to change

Art is all about experimentation. Children often find themselves trying out new ideas or switching directions mid-project. This flexibility teaches them that it's OK to change their minds! For example, if a child decides to turn a landscape into a funky alien world, they're exercising **cognitive flexibility**.

The art of reflection

Finally, engaging with art helps kids develop metacognition – **thinking about their own thinking**. When children reflect on their artwork, they ask questions like, "What do I like about this?" or "How can I make it better?" This self-reflection encourages them to evaluate their choices and learn from their experiences. It's a powerful way for children to become more aware of their thought processes, which leads to improved problem-solving skills.

Dance

 Self-regulation plays a huge part in dancing, especially when learning new steps. It's needed to keep emotions from getting the best of us – usually those of frustration when we practise the same steps over and over again and yet somehow still make the same mistakes. We need it to stay in time with the music, finding the perfect Goldilocks rhythm. Once the steps have been mastered, our brains are flooded with the 'feel-good' hormone dopamine. This allows us to relax, forget about our anxieties and channel our emotions through our movement, promoting overall mental wellbeing.

 Organisation includes setting goals and planning how to achieve them, which are important life skills. With the goal of learning a new dance, time has to be set aside to practise. It's a good reminder of the importance of sequencing and, yes, it is important to get the steps in the correct order.

 Working memory gets a good workout when we dance, since dancing involves memorising and executing specific steps, patterns and routines. Regular dance practice can strengthen working memory capacity, improving the ability to remember and process information effectively. This heightened working memory capacity can have positive implications for various aspects of life, such as academic performance, professional tasks and day-to-day functioning.

 **Attention** and focus are challenged in a unique way when we dance. The coordination required to synchronise movements with music, teammates or partners demands focused attention. Dancing regularly develops our sustained attention and strengthens the ability to filter out distractions, leading to improved concentration and mental focus both on and off the dance floor.

 Thinking flexibly is put to the test through the demands of the choreography. Changing directions, leading with a different arm or leg and changing tempo as the music demands all require us to be constantly adapting, both physically and mentally. The ability to switch between tasks, solve problems and think creatively is certainly enhanced with regular practice.

 **Thinking about our thinking** when dancing begins with self-awareness. When we practise metacognition, we are more conscious of our body's movements and emotional expressions. Good dancers are constantly monitoring their progress and can identify their strengths and weaknesses, enabling them to work on areas that need improvement. Engaging in reflective practices after a dance session or performance helps dancers identify patterns and make informed decisions about future practices and performances – a skill that is useful in many different aspects of our lives.

Music performance

Students need to:

- Use inhibitory control – not play their instrument until the required time.
- Practise emotional regulation – get nerves/excitement under control when performing.
- Stay on task during rehearsals.

- Manage sheet music, instruments, costumes and rehearsal schedules.
- Commit to regular practice.
- Be able to get on and off stage efficiently, without causing unwanted distractions.

- Remember performance cues.
- Remember sequences of notes and lyrics.
- Anticipate changes (for example, tempo) in real time.

- Pay attention to the conductor.
- Follow the music.
- Not get distracted.

- Recover quickly from mistakes or adjust to a missed cue or a change in the group dynamic.
- Improvise when necessary.
- Reframe mindset if things don't go as planned.

- Learn from mistakes.
- Monitor personal progress.
- Evaluate personal performance and areas for improvement.

Project-based learning/inquiry learning

In project-based or inquiry learning, students aren't just learning about a topic – they're learning how to think, plan, adapt and reflect. Some students struggle with protracted tasks, particularly since they often require them to keep track of more than one thing at once. For students who struggle with this, careful scaffolding will be needed to help them complete assignments on time and with the required details.

Students need to:

	• Manage their behaviour and emotions across days or weeks of a long-term project. • Sustain effort over time, handle frustration and keep working even when things get tricky or boring. • Resist the urge to rush the process instead of collecting all the required information. • Example: A student feels overwhelmed by the project timeline but uses a checklist to stay calm and keep going.
	• Set goals. • Plan their tasks, manage resources, keep track of what's done and what's next, organise information and meet deadlines. • Example: A group maps out their roles, keeps notes in a shared folder and tracks progress on a whiteboard.
	• Make connections between prior knowledge and new information. • Hold instructions, project goals and relevant content knowledge in mind as they build, write or present. • Manage multistep tasks. • Example: While making a poster, a student remembers what they learned last week about the water cycle and includes it in their explanation.
	• Sustain attention during research, group discussions and problem solving, even with multiple moving parts or distractions. • Example: A student tunes out noise from another group to focus on revising their part of the script for a class video.

	<ul><li>Adapt when plans change, shift ideas when they get new information and see problems from different angles.</li><li>Analyse and synthesise information from different sources.</li><li>Reassess their perspectives when presented with unexpected findings.</li><li>Example: A group realises their recycled materials won't work for a model and quickly brainstorms a new plan.</li></ul>
	<ul><li>Reflect on what they're learning, how they're learning and what strategies help them work better.</li><li>Example: A student says, "I think we're spending too much time on the visuals – maybe we should focus on getting the facts right first."</li></ul>

Science

Students need to:

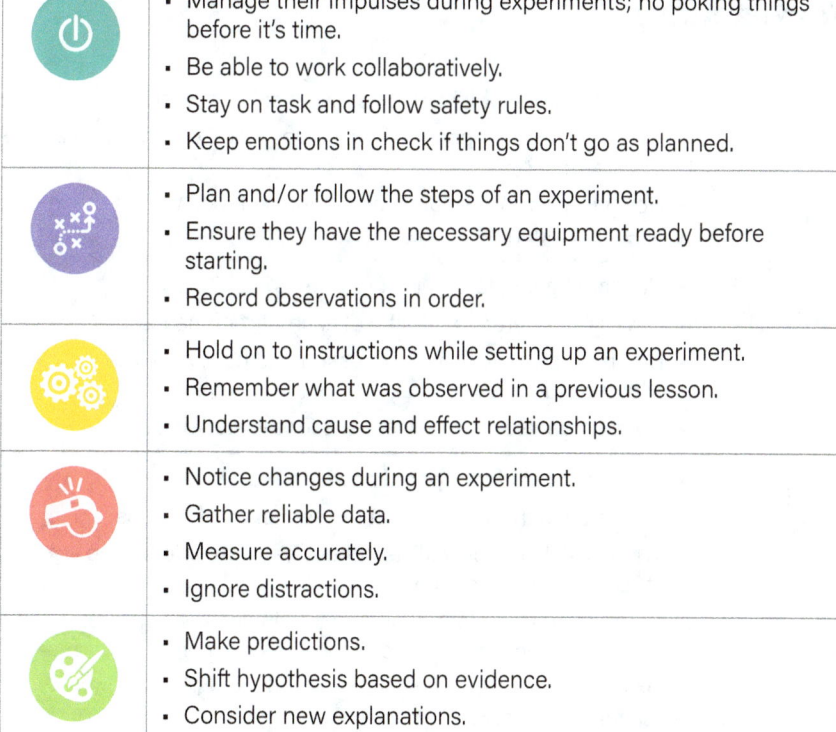

	<ul><li>Monitor the process by asking:<ul><li>"Does my explanation make sense?"</li><li>"What do I still need to find out?"</li><li>"Did we control all the variables?"</li></ul></li><li>Reflect:<ul><li>"What might I do differently next time?"</li></ul></li></ul>

It should now be clear that, regardless of the subject, intentionally developing self-regulation and executive function skills is central to ensuring that learning is retained and embedded in long-term memory. Taking time to reflect on some key questions before teaching can help you unpack both topics and individual lessons, making your instruction more intentional and supporting students in becoming more effective learners. The following questions will help guide your practice...

For teachers

	<ul><li>What strategies will help me stay patient and positive today?</li><li>Have I anticipated possible challenges, and how will I manage them calmly?</li><li>How will I slow down and value thinking time, without trying to give the students the answer straight away?</li></ul>
	<ul><li>How am I going to group the students?</li><li>Have I considered the timing of each part of the lesson?</li><li>Do I have clear goals for this lesson and how will I share them with the students?</li><li>Have I organised some questions for the students?</li></ul>
	<ul><li>What is the students' prior knowledge?</li><li>Where does this lesson sit in the sequence of lessons?</li><li>What visual aids, checklists or cues can I provide to help students hold information in mind?</li><li>How much new information and terminology will I present today, and might this overload the working memory?</li><li>Have I planned opportunities for repetition and practice to reinforce memory?</li></ul>

🔔	• What's my 'hook' to engage students in this material? • How am I going to present this material to reduce extraneous load? • Are there any specific students I need to pay extra attention to?
🎨	• In what ways can I teach this concept? • How can I extend students' thinking? • How can I scaffold students who might be challenged by this material? • Am I open to using student ideas to shape the direction of the lesson?
💭	• How will I check for understanding throughout the lesson? • How will I monitor my students' development and then rework my planning? • What reflection/evaluation tool will I use? • After an assessment, how will I support my students to rectify any issues or mistakes?

If we are aiming to put students in the driving seat, they need to be asking themselves questions, too. Some examples to share with students are as follows...

For students

⏻	• Am I ready to learn? • What do I need to do to get myself in the learning zone? • Am I giving myself time to think before I answer?
📋	• Do I have all the things I need for this lesson? • Where will I sit to ensure I have the best chance of learning? • What is my goal for this lesson? • Did I go to the bathroom before the lesson?
⚙️	• What do I already know about this subject? • When have I done something like this before? • Am I sure I understand what to do?
🔔	• What do I need to pay attention to? • How can I help myself stay focused today? • Am I staying on task or am I getting distracted?

	- Can I be open to changing my plan if I need to? - Am I listening to other people's ideas and considering whether they can help me? - If I'm stuck, can I try a different strategy?
	- What questions can I ask to engage in the learning? - Do I understand what I'm doing, or do I need to ask for help? - Did I try my best? - What could I do differently next time? - What do I need to follow up?

Joke:

"I finally recognised my potential."

"My potential said, 'Great! I'll wait over here while you actually do something.'"

My summary

What are your key takeaways?

How does this chapter relate to what you already know or do?

Chapter 10

Getting started

"Change will not come if we wait for some other person or some other time. We are the one we've been waiting for. We are the change that we seek."

– President Barack Obama

I hope the preceding chapters have helped clarify *why* it's so important to focus on helping students learn *how* to learn. When we understand the value of teaching these skills, we're more likely to prioritise them in our practice. After all, our beliefs strongly influence our behaviours. When we believe something matters, we're far more intentional about making it happen.

As with most things in life, the first step is the hardest – but you must take it if you are going to set students up to be in charge of their learning. Just as "science cannot study what it cannot measure accurately and cannot measure what it does not define" (Durlak & DuPre, 2008), practice cannot improve what it does not target.

First, I would recommend you reflect on your current practices. Chances are, you are already doing many things that will be supporting students to be learning *how* to learn, but maybe this is not at a conscious level. If you are not conscious about what you are doing, then you cannot consciously teach students the necessary strategies and there will be no *intentionality*. What works with the students works with the teachers – we all need to be reflective practitioners.

If you identify something you are already doing, pause and reflect – ask yourself why you are doing it and whether you have ever shared *the why* with the students. If the answer to either of these questions is vague, think what you could change to make your practice more intentional. Focus on one area and aim for a quick win (remember the power of dopamine).

I would suggest a starting point might be to take an objective, non-judgemental look at your classroom – the Classroom Audit on page 163 of the resources section may help you with this. If we get the conditions right for learning, we are already setting ourselves and our students up for success. Be honest about your relationships with *all* your students. Which ones might be slipping through the net? Which ones are making it harder, or more challenging, to like? Make these students your immediate priority!

The goal of the SOWATT approach is to weave its elements into every lesson, every day, giving both teachers and students regular opportunities to practise them. Even in primary schools, the pressure to 'cover the curriculum' can be intense, with teachers expected to write learning intentions and identify success criteria based on content. Too often, this leads to binary thinking: focusing either on content or on skill development.

In reality, we don't need to choose, and in fact, we can't afford to. The challenge is to plan intentionally for both. Every lesson or activity should, therefore, carry two parallel goals: a content goal and an executive function goal. If we are serious about developing executive functions (with the longer-term aim of putting students in the driver's seat), we must plan for them deliberately and make them visible to students.

Just as importantly, we must show that we value both. When students see us prioritising their ability to manage attention, plan, shift perspective and persist alongside learning fractions or phonics, they quickly understand the message: these skills matter, too.

This dual focus changes the way we think about assessment. It's not just about tracking whether a student can recall facts, apply a formula or write a persuasive sentence. It's also about noticing whether they are demonstrating persistence, flexibility or self-regulation in the process.

Embedding executive function instruction within everyday content teaching reinforces the idea that *students are active agents in their own learning*. This does not mean all six elements will appear in every lesson. SOWATT is not hierarchical or linear – you can dip in and out of any element as needed, and often, working on one inevitably touches two or three others because they are interconnected. It also doesn't mean working mechanically through every strategy on the list. Even small, purposeful adjustments, thoughtfully selected for your context, can make a powerful difference, and often teaching *fewer strategies more deeply* leads to stronger outcomes.

A starting point might be focusing on attention, since without it, no learning will take place. This then needs to be intentionally included in every lesson. Essentially, you are looking to build good habits. In addition, most primary school classes will be able to find some time during the week for some explicit instruction on SOWATT and *learning to learn*. It does not have to be long: 20–30 minutes each week explicitly teaching students a SOWATT element and linking this to a strategy which will be practised during the coming week is a good way of ensuring you get in the habit of planning, implementing and evaluating on a regular basis. Involving students in the process promotes their active engagement in the learning process and increases their own self-awareness of their strengths and challenges.

You will have noticed that in the 'Mindset and Motivation' sections for teachers, I have included a reminder to 'Find the fun!' This is important for both the teacher and the student because, as you already know, learning and emotions go hand in hand. Learning can't get processed in the prefrontal cortex when we are anxious or preoccupied with other concerns. This links to my earlier point about getting your classroom environment right. It is also a reminder that teachers are as unique as the students – we each have our own personalities and preferences. The SOWATT approach is 'Top Down' in the sense that it is your responsibility to make a difference to students' learning by intentionally developing the SOWATT skills, but it is 'Bottom Up' because you get to choose the strategies that you think will work best for you in your context.

Educational research clearly shows us that context matters. Remember that not every strategy will work well in every situation. This is why teaching is such a skill – there is not a one-size-fits-all approach. It's also why Marzano (2017) refers to teaching as being both an 'Art' and a 'Science'. While science might provide principles on which to base our teaching, effective teachers and learners are skilled at the art of knowing which strategies to employ in specific situations or contexts. I encourage you, therefore, to be creative. As a practitioner, I know the joy of having the autonomy and trust to run with an idea and make it my own.

A word of caution: remember that, often, we give students the tools and there's a belief that they know how to use them. Explicit instruction as to how to use the tools is required and, of course, practice. Just because you pick up a set of golf clubs from the side of the road, doesn't make you a golfer! Developing the skills to learn how to learn develops with time and practice.

All staff from art teachers to sports coaches should understand how underdeveloped executive functions can impact learning in their subject areas. This shared awareness empowers them to recognise and respond to students' needs more effectively, and perhaps even more importantly, enables a common language for professional dialogue across disciplines. Breaking down silos between subject specialists gives students the best chance of receiving consistent support.

For example, a student may demonstrate excellent impulse control during sport, but struggle with the same skill when working through an English comprehension task. When teachers connect these behaviours across contexts, students can begin to recognise their own strengths and apply them more broadly. This kind of cross-subject reinforcement builds self-efficacy, and when students believe they can succeed, they're more likely to rise to the challenge. Self-efficacy, after all, can become a powerful self-fulfilling prophecy.

Planning

This brings us back to the eighth principle underpinning the SOWATT model – *intentionality*. Without it, we are just hoping for the best and have no structure to reflect on our practice. Plan activities, plan transitions, plan how you are going to check for understanding, plan observations of individual students and reflect on what you see.

Whether you are observing a group of students or a colleague, plan what you want to focus on beforehand. If you don't, you run the risk of being so absorbed in the lesson that it's difficult to establish exactly what you saw and heard. Select something that is manageable, otherwise your attention will be switching from one thing to another, and we already know from Chapter 6 that this is not an effective use of our time!

Before giving students any task, take a moment to consider the cognitive demands. Have another look at the questions for teachers in Chapter 9.

As discussed in Chapter 1, it is important to provide students with timely feedback both during and after tasks, to support their learning. Instead of simply asking, "How do you feel?" after introducing new content, consider asking, "How confident are you that you know this?" This question invites students to reflect on their understanding more intentionally.

Follow this with a brief retrieval practice activity to help students compare their perceived confidence with their actual performance. This can often highlight the distinction between *feeling* effective and *being* effective. While perceived and actual self-efficacy are distinct, they are deeply interconnected. A strong sense of self-efficacy can boost motivation and enhance performance, while successful performance, in turn, reinforces confidence and belief in one's abilities. For optimal learning, both must be nurtured. Students need to develop not only the skills to perform a task but also the belief that they can. Research by Zimmerman (2000) found that self-regulated learners are better able to calibrate their self-efficacy beliefs with their actual performance. His work also highlights that self-efficacy is highly malleable and can be strengthened through targeted strategies such as timely feedback, reflective practices and guided learning experiences.

A whole-school approach is obviously the best way forward, as it creates a community of learners from which to learn and to receive support. It also provides the opportunity to create a shared language around your goals. Having a shared clarity around terminology is also imperative to avoid confusion among both the staff and the students. The Year 1 teacher's understanding of metacognition needs to be the same as the Year 6 teacher's – it just might look different in practice as strategies are tailored to different age groups. However, if you are a lone voice or in a minority, don't feel overwhelmed – view it as an opportunity to conduct some 'action research'. Implement a couple of strategies from one or two of the SOWATT elements and see what happens as a result. Set clear success criteria from the outset so you can gather evidence and share your findings with the wider community at the end of the term.

One approach that I have found useful in my practice is the Micro-Project (thank you, Jared Cooney Horvath, 2019). The idea behind a Micro-Project is that you choose something you would like to focus on in your classroom, preferably something specific and contained, for example, students being ready at the beginning of a lesson. This is one tiny aspect of organisation; if you want your students to be better organised, then you need to deconstruct the concept into individual skills. Once identified, you then determine your success criteria. In this example, success might look like this: All students have the necessary resources on their table before the lesson begins, there are no unnecessary items or distractions present and students have used the bathroom beforehand, so they're ready to engage from the outset. The next step is to identify what you need to do in order to support the students to be able to achieve this goal, which in this example will require sharing explicit expectations for the start of each lesson and an identified timeframe that you would expect students to be ready, such as four minutes. You may decide to cue the students into this with the aid of a short piece of music. It is also important to share the *why* with students, so they understand that this routine is necessary so that everyone is ready to learn – it is not because Mr Simmons has unilaterally decided to do so. This is consistently monitored for a period of two weeks – just 10 school days. At the end of this period, you review what you are seeing with your students and decide whether to continue for another two weeks. The strength of the Micro-Project is that it increases intentionality, improves accountability and the two- to four-week timeframe makes it manageable.

Another approach, which is very similar to Micro-Projects, and one that you may already be familiar with, is Teaching Sprints (Breakspear & Jones, 2020). Each sprint typically runs for two to four weeks with the aim of improving teaching effectiveness and student learning incrementally. Teachers base their chosen strategy on research, but test and adapt it in their context. The goal is to bridge the gap between theory and classroom reality.

To encourage students to take more responsibility for their learning, consider introducing 'Learning Journals'. These may take a variety of forms: written notebooks, digital logs, voice recordings or even drawings. It all depends on the age and needs of your students. The idea is to give students a space to reflect on what they're learning, how they're learning and how it connects to what they already know.

Learning Journals help students become more aware of their own thinking. They encourage reflection, which builds confidence, supports memory and helps students understand themselves as learners. Journals can also give teachers useful insights into students' ideas, challenges and progress.

To get students started, you might offer some simple prompts like:

- "What did I find easy or tricky today?"
- "What helped me learn something new?"
- "What questions do I still have?"
- "How did I feel about my learning today?"
- "What's one thing I want to try next time?"

Used regularly, Learning Journals can become a powerful habit that supports growth, curiosity and responsibility for learning.

Mastery takes time – and usually longer than you'd expect. As Douglas Hofstadter (1979) famously noted, "It always takes longer than you expect, even when you take into account Hofstadter's Law." Just as students need to practise the skills that support learning, so too must teachers. Ideally, this journey is shared – collaborating with colleagues not only sparks new ideas but also enables collective problem solving and deeper professional insight.

To paraphrase Michael Fullen (2025), one of the most influential thought leaders in education reform, "hold fast to knowledge that change happens from the inside out, not the outside in". I would encourage you to gather evidence in order to 'intrigue the top' and flip the traditional top-down model. Real, lasting change in education often starts at the grassroots level, with passionate teachers and school leaders who are trying innovative practices in their classrooms and communities.

How will you know if you are making a difference?

Our memories are not infallible; they are constantly shaped by emotion, context and time, making them more a reconstruction of the past than a perfect record of it. Every time we recall an event, our brains reconstruct it, filling in gaps, adjusting details and sometimes even reshaping entire narratives based on our current beliefs, emotions or the stories we've heard from others. We also tend to remember things in ways that align with our existing views of ourselves or the world. Remember, you don't need an abundance of resources – what matters most is not only your understanding of how students learn, but also your ability to guide that process. Like all things in education, supporting students to learn how to learn needs to be continually reviewed and monitored so that you know your work is effective. Two questions to ask yourself are:

- *How is my teaching today impacting students' self-regulation and executive function development?*
- *What is my evidence?*

With these in mind, here are some suggestions of data sources for you to consider, preferably at the start of your executive function journey:

- Reflective journals – both teacher and students
- A common language emerging
- Student self-assessment and self-efficacy
- Self-correction or strategising
- Observing new skills being used in appropriate contexts

- Grades/test scores

By intentionally developing the six SOWATT skills, we support our students in driving their own learning, empowering them to become confident, self-regulated learners equipped with a rich toolkit of strategies to navigate and embrace new learning independently. In a world defined by constant change and uncertainty, this is one of the greatest gifts we can offer: not just igniting a passion for learning but equipping them with the skills to pursue it. This powerful combination lays the foundation for lifelong growth, personal development and a life of purpose and possibility.

Final word...

> *"They say you can't teach an old dog new tricks... luckily, lifelong learners aren't dogs!"*

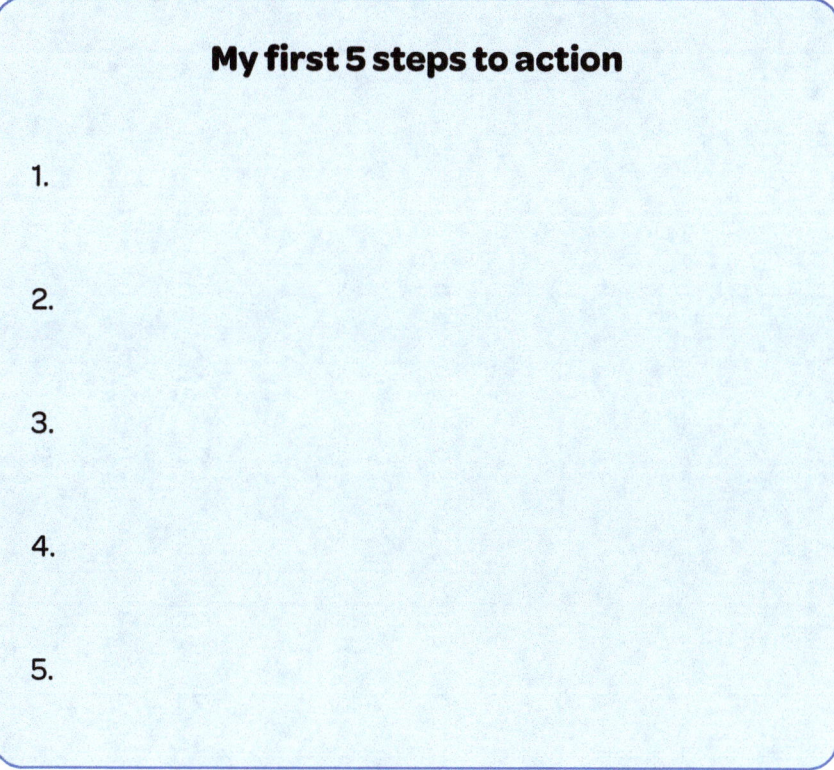

My first 5 steps to action

1.

2.

3.

4.

5.

References

Australian Bureau of Statistics. (2024). Schools. ABS. https://www.abs.gov.au/statistics/people/education/schools/latest-release

Australian Curriculum, Assessment and Reporting Authority (ACARA). (n.d.). https://www.acara.edu.au/curriculum

Bjork, E. L., & Bjork, R. A. (2014). Making things hard on yourself, but in a good way: Creating desirable difficulties to enhance learning. In M. A. Gernsbacher & J. Pomerantz (Eds.), *Psychology and the real world: Essays illustrating fundamental contributions to society (2nd edition)*, 59-68. Worth Publishers.

Blair, C., & Raver, C. C. (2015). School Readiness and Self-Regulation: A Developmental Psychobiological Approach. *Annual Review of Psychology, 66*, 711-731. https://doi.org/10.1146/annurev-psych-010814-015221

Brackett, M. A. (2019). *Permission to Feel: Unlocking the Power of Emotions to Help Our Kids, Ourselves, and Our Society Thrive*. Celadon Books.

Braund, H. (2022). Thinking about Kindergarten thinking: A mixed methods study. *Frontiers in Psychology, 13*, 933541.

Breakspear, S., & Jones, B. R. (2020). *Teaching Sprints: How Overloaded Educators Can Keep Getting Better*. Corwin.

Burman, J. T., Green, C. D., & Shanker, S. (2015). On the meanings of self-regulation: Digital Humanities in service of conceptual clarity. *Child Development, 86*(5), 1507-1521.

Center on the Developing Child at Harvard University. (2016). *From Best Practices to Breakthrough Impacts: A science-based approach to building a more promising future for young children and families*. Retrieved from https://developingchild.harvard.edu/resources/report/best-practices-breakthrough-impacts/

Cohen, G. L., Steele, C. M., & Ross, L. D. (1999). The mentor's dilemma: Providing critical feedback across the racial divide. *Personality and Social Psychology Bulletin, 25*(10), 1302-1318.

Csíkszentmihályi, M., & LeFevre, J. (1989). Optimal experience in work and leisure. *Journal of Personality and Social Psychology, 56*(5), 815–822.

Curcio, G., Ferrara, M., & De Gennaro, L. (2006). Sleep loss, learning capacity and academic performance. *Sleep Medicine Reviews, 10*(5), 323–337.

Darling-Hammond, L. (2000). Teacher Quality and Student Achievement. *Education Policy Analysis Archives, 8,* 1.

Department for Education, UK. (n.d.) https://www.gov.uk/government/organisations/department-for-education

Diamond, A. (2016). Why improving and assessing executive functions early in life is critical. In J. A. Griffin, P. McCardle, & L. S. Freund (Eds.), *Executive function in preschool-age children: Integrating measurement, neurodevelopment, and translational research,* 11–43. American Psychological Association.

Diamond, A., & Lee, K. (2011). Interventions shown to Aid Executive Function Development in Children 4–12 years old. *Science, 333*(6045), 959–964.

Diamond, A., & Ling, D. S. (2016). Conclusions about interventions, programs, and approaches for improving executive functions that appear justified and those that, despite much hype, do not. *Developmental Cognitive Neuroscience, 18,* 34–48.

Dignath, C., & Büttner, G. (2008). Components of fostering self-regulated learning among students. A meta-analysis on intervention studies at primary and secondary school level. *Metacognition and Learning, 3*(3), 231–264.

du Castel, B. (2015). Pattern activation/recognition theory of mind. *Frontiers in Computational Neuroscience, 9,* Article 90.

Duckworth, A., & Gross, J. J. (2014). Self-Control and Grit: Related but Separable Determinants of Success. *Current Directions in Psychological Science, 23*(5), 319–325.

Durlak, J. A., & DuPre, E. P. (2008). Implementation matters: a review of research on the influence of implementation on program outcomes and the factors affecting implementation. *American Journal of Community Psychology, 41*(3), 327–350.

Dweck, C. (2015). Carol Dweck Revisits the 'Growth Mindset'. *Education Week, 35*(5), 20–24.

Eberhart, J., Ingendahl, F., & Bryce, D. (2025). Are metacognition interventions in young children effective? Evidence from a series of meta-analyses. *Metacognition and Learning, 20*(1), 7.

Edossa, A. K., Schroeders, U., Weinert, S., & Artelt, C. (2018). The development of emotional and behavioral self-regulation and their effects on academic achievement in childhood. *International Journal of Behavioral Development, 42*(2), 192–202.

Education Endowment Foundation (EEF). (2018). *Metacognition and Self-Regulated Learning Guidance Report.* https://educationendowment foundation.org.uk/education-evidence/guidance-reports/metacognition

Fisher, D., & Frey, N. (2021). *Better Learning Through Structured Teaching: A Framework for the Gradual Release of Responsibility.* ASCD.

Flavell, J. H. (1979). Metacognition and cognitive monitoring: A new area of cognitive–developmental inquiry. *American Psychologist, 34*(10), 906–911.

Frith, C. D., & Frith, U. (2007). Social cognition in humans. *Current Biology, 17*(16), R724-R732.

Fullan, M. (2025). *The New Meaning of Educational Change (Sixth Edition).* New York: Teachers College Press.

Garon-Carrier, G., Boivin, M., Guay, F., Kovas, Y., Dionne, G., Lemelin, J. P., Séguin, J. R., Vitaro, F., & Tremblay, R. E. (2016). Intrinsic Motivation and Achievement in Mathematics in Elementary School: A Longitudinal Investigation of Their Association. *Child Development, 87*(1), 165–175.

Government of Canada. (n.d.) https://www.canada.ca/en/employment-social-development/programs/agenda-2030/quality-education

Hanushek, E. A., & Woessmann, L. (2015). *The Knowledge Capital of Nations: Education and the Economics of Growth.* MIT Press.

Hanushek, E. A., & Woessmann, L. (2021). Education and Economic Growth. In *Oxford Research Encyclopedia of Economics and Finance.*

Hattie. J. (2025). Dean's Lecture Series, The University of Melbourne, Recorded 27 August.

Hattie, J., & Timperley, H. (2007). *The Power of Feedback. Review of Educational Research, 77*(1), 81–112.

Heckman, J. J. (2011). The Economics of Inequality: The Value of Early Childhood Education. *American Educator, 35*(1), 31.

Hendrick, C., & MacPherson, R. (Eds.). (2017). *What does this look like in the classroom? Bridging the gap between research and practice.* John Catt Educational Ltd.

Hofstadter, D. R. (1979). *Gödel, Escher, Bach: An Eternal Golden Braid.* Basic Books.

Horvath, J. C. (2019). *Micro-Projects: A practical framework for teachers.* Learning Made Easy Global. Retrieved from https://d1aettbyeyfilo.cloudfront.net/lmeglobal/7642755_1580228488539MICRO_PROJECTS_BOOK_-_JARED_COONEY_HORVATH.pdf

Howard-Jones, P. (2019). *The plastic brain.* Science of Learning Portal. International Bureau of Education / UNESCO.

Howard, S. J., & Vasseleu, E. (2020). Self-Regulation and Executive Function Longitudinally Predict Advanced Learning in Preschool. *Frontiers in Psychology, 11*, 49.

Jacob, R., & Parkinson, J. (2015). The Potential for School-Based Interventions That Target Executive Function to Improve Academic Achievement: A Review. *Review of Educational Research, 85*(4), 512–552.

Keable, L. (2025). Metacognition in Practice. LinkedIn Blog.

Kitil, M. J., Diamond, A., Guhn, M., & Schonert-Reichl, K. A. (2025). Longitudinal relations of executive functions to academic achievement and wellbeing in adolescence. In *Frontiers in Education, 10*, 1573107. Frontiers Media SA.

Le Cunff, A.-L. (2025). *Tiny Experiments: How to Live Freely in a Goal-Obsessed World.* Ness Labs Press.

Leonard, H. (2023). *Longitudinal Associations Between Early Parenting and Adolescent Allostatic Load: Examining the Mediating and Moderating Role of Child Delay of Gratification.* Doctoral dissertation, University of Oregon.

Lovell, O. (2020). *Sweller's Cognitive Load Theory in Action.* John Catt Educational.

Madanipour, P., Garvis, S., Cohrssen, C., & Pendergast, D. (2025). Early childhood teachers' understanding of executive functions and strategies employed to facilitate them. In *Frontiers in Education, 9*, 1488410. Frontiers Media SA.

Marzano, R. J. (2017). *The New Art and Science of Teaching: More Than Fifty New Instructional Strategies for Academic Success.* Solution Tree Press.

McClelland, M. M., & Cameron, C. E. (2019). Developing together: The role of executive function and motor skills in children's early academic lives. *Early Childhood Research Quarterly, 46*, 142–151.

McCoy, D. C., & Sabol, T. J. (2025). Overcoming the streetlight effect: Shining light on the foundations of learning and development in early childhood. *American Psychologist, 80*(2), 135–147.

McCoy, J. M., & Evans, G. W. (2002). The potential role of the physical environment in fostering creativity. *Creativity Research Journal, 14*(3-4), 409-426.

Mercer, N., & Howe, C. (2012). Explaining the dialogic processes of teaching and learning: The value and potential of sociocultural theory. *Learning, Culture and Social Interaction, 1*(1), 12-21.

Ministry of Education and Culture, Finland. (n.d.). https://okm.fi/en/

Ministry of Education, New Zealand. (n.d.). https://www.education.govt.nz/

Moffitt, T. E., Arseneault, L., Belsky, D., Dickson, N., Hancox, R. J., Harrington, H., Houts, R., Poulton, R., Roberts, B. W., Ross, S., Sears, M. R., Thomson, W. M., & Caspi, A. (2011). A gradient of childhood self-control predicts health, wealth, and public safety. *Proceedings of the National Academy of Sciences, 108*(7), 2693-2698.

New South Wales Department of Education. (2018). Centre for Education Statistics and Evaluation. https://education.nsw.gov.au/about-us/education-data-and-research/cese/publications/practical-guides-for-educators/cognitive-load-theory-in-practice

Ohtani, K., & Hisasaka, T. (2018). Beyond intelligence: a meta-analytic review of the relationship among metacognition, intelligence, and academic performance. *Metacognition and Learning, 13*(2), 179-212.

Organisation for Economic Co-operation and Development (OECD). (2025). *Trends Shaping Education 2025*, OECD Publishing.

Pearson, P. D., & Gallagher, M. C. (1983). The gradual release of responsibility model of instruction. *Contemporary Educational Psychology, 8*(3).

Peterson, L., & Peterson, M. J. (1959). Short-term retention of individual verbal items. *Journal of Experimental Psychology, 58*(3), 193-198.

Petersen, S. E., & Posner, M. I. (2012). The attention system of the human brain: 20 years after. *Annual Review of Neuroscience, 35*(1), 73-89.

Psacharopoulos, G., & Patrinos, H. A. (2018). Returns to investment in education: a decennial review of the global literature. *Education Economics, 26*(5), 445-458.

Raver, C. C. (2002). Emotions Matter: Making the Case for the Role of Young Children's Emotional Development for Early School Readiness. SRCD. *Social Policy Report, 16*(3), 3-19.

Raver, C. C., Jones, S. M., Li-Grining, C., Zhai, F., Metzger, M., & Solomon, B. (2011). CSRP's Impact on low-Income preschoolers' Preacademic Skills: Self-Regulation as a Mediating Mechanism. SRCD. *Child Development, 82*(1), 362-378.

Rodríguez, S., González-Suárez, R., Vieites, T., Piñeiro, I., & Díaz-Freire, F. M. (2022). Self-Regulation and Students Well-Being: A Systematic Review 2010–2020. *Sustainability, 14*(4), 2346.

Rogers, C., & Thomas, M. S. (2022). *Educational Neuroscience: The Basics.* Routledge.

Ryan, R. M., & Deci, E. L. (2000). Self-Determination Theory and the Facilitation of Intrinsic Motivation, Social Development, and Well-Being. *American Psychologist, 55*(1), 68–78.

Schunk, D., Meece, J., & Pintrich, P. (2014). *Motivation in Education: Theory, Research, and Applications* (Fourth Edition). Pearson.

Sherrington, T., & Caviglioli, O. (2022). *Teaching WalkThrus 3: Five-Step Guides to Instructional Coaching.* John Catt Educational.

Shonkoff, J. P., & Phillips, D. A. (Eds.) (2000). *From Neurons to Neighborhoods: The Science of Early Childhood Development.* The National Academies of Sciences, Engineering, and Medicine.

Simon, A. J., Gallen, C. L., Ziegler, D. A., Mishra, J., Marco, E. J., Anguera, J. A., & Gazzaley, A. (2023). Quantifying attention span across the lifespan. *Frontiers in Cognition, 2,* 1207428. Frontiers Media SA.

Slavin, R. E. (2020). How evidence-based reform will transform research and practice in education. *Educational Psychologist, 55*(1), 21–31.

Spengler, M., Damian, R. I., & Roberts, B. W. (2018). How you behave in school predicts life success above and beyond family background, broad traits, and cognitive ability. *Journal of Personality and Social Psychology, 114*(4), 620–636.

Sweller, J., Ayres, P., Kalyuga, S. (2011). Cognitive Load Theory. Springer.

Timmons, K., Pelletier, J., & Corter, C. (2016). Understanding children's self-regulation within different classroom contexts. *Early Child Development and Care, 186*(2), 249–267.

U.S. Department of Education. (n.d.). https://www.ed.gov/

Veenman, M. V. J., Van Hout-Wolters, B., & Afflerbach, P. (2006). Metacognition and learning: Conceptual and methodological considerations. *Metacognition and Learning, 1*(1), 3–14.

Vygotsky, L. S. (1978). *Mind in Society: The Development of Higher Psychological Processes* (M. Cole, V. John-Steiner, S. Scribner, & E. Souberman, Eds. & Trans.). Harvard University Press. (Original work published 1934.)

Whitebread, D., Coltman, P., Pasternak, D. P., Sangster, C., Grau, V., Bingham, S., Almeqdad, Q., & Demetriou, D. (2009). The development of two observational tools for assessing metacognition and self-regulated learning in young children. *Metacognition and Learning, 4*(1), 63–85.

Willingham, D. T. (2007). Critical Thinking: Why Is It So Hard to Teach? American Federation of Teachers. *American Educator*, 8–19.

World Economic Forum (WEF). (2025). *The Future of Jobs Report 2025.* https://www.weforum.org/reports/the-future-of-jobs-report-2025/

Xu, C., Huizinga, M., Tekelia Ekubagewargies, D., Soetaert, J., Van Den Noortgate, W., & Baeyens, D. (2024). The relation between teacher-student interaction and executive function performance in children: A cross-cultural meta-analysis. *Educational Psychologist, 59*(3), 195–215.

Zelazo, P. D., & Carlson, S. M. (2012). Hot and Cool Executive Function in Childhood and Adolescence: Development and Plasticity. *Child Development Perspectives, 6*(4), 354–360.

Zhai, N., Huang, Y., Ma, X., & Chen, J. (2023). Can Reflective Interventions Improve Students' Academic Achievement? A Meta-analysis. *Thinking Skills and Creativity, 49*(4), 101373.

Zhou, Y., Curtis, C. E., Sreenivasan, K. K., & Fougnie, D. (2022). Common Neural Mechanisms Control Attention and Working Memory. *Journal of Neuroscience, 42*(37), 7110–7120.

Zimmerman, B. J. (2000). Self-Efficacy: An Essential Motive to Learn. *Contemporary Educational Psychology, 25*(1), 82–91.

Zimmerman, B. J. (2002). Becoming a Self-Regulated Learner: An Overview. *Theory Into Practice, 41*(2), 64–70.

Zimmerman, B. J. (2020). Self-Regulated Learning and Academic Achievement. *Educational Psychology Review, 32*(2), 321–335.

Zohar, A., & Barzilai, S. (2013). A review of research on metacognition in science education: current and future directions. *Studies in Science Education, 49*(2), 121–169.

Acknowledgements

After many years of teaching and learning alongside children, families and colleagues, I know that education is never a solo journey. This book is no exception. It reflects not only my own experiences as a lifelong learner, but also the wisdom, generosity and encouragement of those who have walked this path with me.

To my colleagues, past and present, thank you for challenging my thinking and sharing your practice so openly. To my students, young and old, you have been my greatest teachers. To my family, Ken, Lorna and Katherine, you are my biggest supporters, thank you for your patience, love and steady belief in me. You are the foundation that made this work possible.

Huge thanks to the incredible team who helped bring all the pieces together. To my amazing critical friends, Russell Kaplan, Taryn Stark and Kaisu Tonkyra, thank you for selflessly reading the drafts and adding your reflections. To the team at Amba Press, particularly Alicia Cohen for her unwavering support and encouragement, and Rica Dearman for her sharp eye and attention to detail during the editing stages. Without you, these ideas would still be scattered across notebooks and classrooms rather than bound in these pages.

This book is the product of many hands, many minds and many years. I am deeply grateful to everyone who has been part of the journey.

Learning is rarely a solitary pursuit. SOWATT can we do? Learn, grow and move forward together.

About the author

Rosalyn has spent her career following her natural curiosity and love of learning, which has taken her across Europe, Asia, the Americas and now Australia. Along the way, she has embraced roles as classroom teacher, head teacher, advisor and researcher – each experience deepening her belief that it is the teachers in the classroom who hold the greatest power to change lives.

Her master's research explored teacher professional development and the alignment between personal and school-wide goals. Building on this, her PhD examined how teachers can nurture executive function and self-regulation – skills that underpin lifelong success. Today, she works primarily with teachers to embed these critical skills into everyday practice, while still stepping back into classrooms when called upon. Staying close to 'the chalk face' not only grounds her work in reality, but also allows her to refine, test and intentionally enhance the executive functions of students in real time.

Curiosity shapes her life beyond the classroom – whether she's gathering friends around the dinner table (while her husband happily handles the cooking), chasing parkruns in far-flung places or exploring Victoria with Harley, her spirited Hungarian Vizsla.

For further help with supporting students
to drive their learning, please contact
Rosalyn via her website:

www.sowattlearning.com

Resources

SOWATT links to Personal and Social Capability	156
SOWATT links to Critical and Creative Thinking Capability	157
SOWATT links to the IB Learner Profile	158
Teaching students about their brain and SOWATT	159
Student self-reflection: *Thinking about myself as a learner*	161
Classroom Audit through the SOWATT lens	163
Teacher checklist of student learning	164
Teaching SOWATT to primary students – sample activities	166
Examples of 3 × 3 grid for retrieval practice	168
Group work self-assessment: Lower primary	169
Group work self-assessment rubric – collaboration and contribution: Upper primary	170
Question matrix	171
Examples of metacognitive prompts	172
Metacognitive prompts and questions for writing a persuasive speech	173
Embedding metacognition	175

SOWATT links to Personal and Social Capability

Personal and social capability skills are addressed in all learning areas and at every stage of a student's schooling. This enables teachers to plan for the teaching of targeted skills specific to an individual's learning needs to provide access to and engagement with the learning areas.

Self-awareness	Self-management	Social awareness	Social management
recognise emotions recognise personal qualities and achievements understand themselves as learners develop reflective practice	express emotions appropriately develop self-discipline and set goals work independently and show initiative become confident, resilient and adaptable	empathy relational awareness community awareness	communicate effectively work collaboratively make decisions negotiate and resolve conflict develop leadership skills

SOWATT links to Critical and Creative Thinking Capability

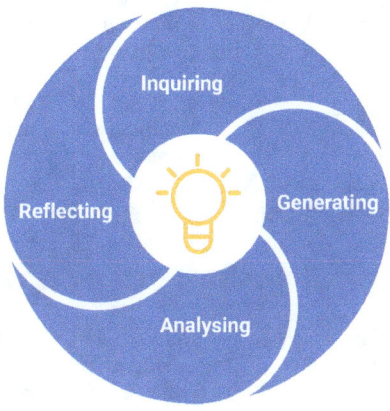

Activities that foster critical and creative thinking should include both independent and collaborative tasks, and entail some sort of transition or tension between ways of thinking. They should be challenging and engaging, and contain approaches that are within the ability range of the learners, but also challenge them to think logically, reason, be open-minded, seek alternatives, tolerate ambiguity, inquire into possibilities, be innovative risk-takers and use their imagination.

Inquiring, identifying, exploring and organising information and ideas	Generating ideas, possibilities and actions	Analysing, synthesising and evaluating reasoning and procedures	Reflecting on thinking and process
pose questions identify, process and evaluate information put ideas into action organise and process information	create possibilities consider alternatives put ideas into action	interpret concepts and problems draw conclusions and provide reasons evaluate actions and outcomes	think about thinking reflect on processes transfer knowledge into new contexts

SOWATT links to the IB Learner Profile

SOWATT element	Core function	Aligned IB Learner Profile attributes	Connection
Self-regulation	Managing emotions, impulses and behaviours to achieve goals.	**Balanced Principled Reflective**	Self-regulated learners maintain emotional and cognitive balance, act with integrity and reflect on their choices – mirroring the IB emphasis on balance and principled action.
Organisation	Planning, prioritising and structuring tasks effectively.	**Thinkers Knowledgeable Reflective**	Organised learners think critically about how to manage their learning and reflect on strategies, demonstrating knowledge application and careful planning.
Working memory	Holding and manipulating information for problem solving and reasoning.	**Thinkers Inquirers**	Strong working memory supports inquiry, reasoning and critical thinking – key attributes of IB Thinkers and Inquirers.
Attention	Sustaining focus, filtering distractions and adapting focus when needed.	**Balanced Caring Principled**	Focused learners can engage deeply, show consideration for others and act responsibly – aligning with balance, care and principled behaviour.
Thinking flexibly	Adapting thinking, seeing multiple perspectives and problem solving creatively.	**Open-minded Risk-takers Thinkers**	Flexible thinkers embrace diverse perspectives, take intellectual risks and approach problems creatively – echoing open-minded and risk-taker qualities.
Thinking about thinking	Reflecting on one's own thinking and learning processes.	**Reflective Inquirers Communicators**	Metacognitive learners evaluate their understanding, ask questions and articulate their thinking, connecting directly to reflection, inquiry and communication.

Teaching students about their brain and SOWATT

Unit	Lesson	Objective: students will...
The brain	Parts of the brain	- Understand that they have a brain that allows them to think, feel and make decisions about how they behave
- Understand that the structure of the brain changes in response to the environment and experiences – it is malleable
- Know that the **amygdala** is responsible for our emotions and the role it can play in learning
- Know that the **prefrontal cortex** is responsible for reasoning and executive functions – it is still maturing and malleable
- Understand the role of the **Reticular Activating System** (RAS) – as a filter and link to growth mindset/self-efficacy
	Looking after our brains	- Understand that the brain uses a lot of energy and that's why learning can sometimes feel hard
- Understand that learning takes practice – use the analogy of walking through a field of long grass – practice builds strong neural connections
- Understand the importance of looking after our brains: getting enough sleep, good food, exercise, challenging it
Mindsets	Growth mindset	- Understand the importance of a growth mindset
- Focus on the process in addition to the end product
- Understand the importance of effort
- Link to RAS
- Understand mistakes are part of learning
Motivation	Its role in learning	- Understand it is the reason we try to learn or do something
- Understand why it matters
- What helps motivation?
Self-regulation	What/why/how	- Know why it's an important skill to master not only to use in their learning, but in life
- Learn some strategies to help themselves self-regulate

Unit	Lesson	Objective: students will...
Organisation	What/why/how	- Link to memory - Be able to set learning goals - Be ready to learn – equipment ready, toileted - Understand the importance of organising: time, resources, ideas, information, space - Learn some strategies to develop organisational skills
Working memory	What/why/how	- Appreciate its limited capacity - Know the importance of linking to prior knowledge – schemas - Automatise routine tasks, for example, multiplication tables, correct formation of letters - Learn some strategies to support working memory
Attention	What/why/how	- Understand the importance of paying attention - Understand the concept of sustained attention - Increase their self-awareness of when distracted - Learn some strategies to help maintain focus/get back on focus
Thinking flexibly	What/why/how	- Problem solve – same problem, different strategies - Know the benefits of shifting mindsets - Practise seeing different perspectives - Practise generating different viewpoints and link to empathy
Thinking about thinking	What/why/how	- Acts like a bridge between the SOWATT elements - Develop their self-awareness of learning strengths and weaknesses - Understand the importance of monitoring their progress through tasks - Be able to reflect on a task and identify the strategies used to complete it - Understand the importance of learning from mistakes

Student self-reflection: *Thinking about myself as a learner*

Answer how well each statement describes you in general (both at home and at school). Score each answer as follows:

- **0** Doesn't describe me at all
- **1** A bit like me
- **2** Describes me pretty well
- **3** Definitely describes me

		Score	
		School	Home
	I find it difficult to stop and think before acting		
	I often interrupt conversations or speak out of turn		
	I would rather play than wait until my work is done		
	I often have difficulty keeping my cool when someone annoys me		
	I often have difficulty with quiet or seated activities		
	My personal work area is messy		
	I am disorganised		
	I don't prioritise or plan my day		
	I often waste a lot of time doing nothing		
	I don't usually pack my own schoolbag		
	I have trouble remembering things I want to do		
	I lose or misplace things		
	I have trouble remembering instructions		
	I have difficulty completing a task that has three or more steps		
	I often lose track of the plot when I am reading		

		Score	
		School	Home
🛑	I often don't listen when a teacher is giving instructions		
	I daydream/space out (I think about other things rather than work)		
	I often try to do more than one thing at a time		
	If I get distracted, I have difficulty getting myself back on task		
	When I start a task, I often give up before finishing it		
🎨	When I'm stuck, I find it difficult to think of another solution to the problem		
	I get frustrated when things don't go according to plan		
	I find it difficult when I can't get what I want when working/playing in a group		
	I don't like change		
	I find it difficult to think of things to do in my spare time		
💭	I don't know what to do to improve my learning		
	I don't pay attention to people's faces when I am speaking to them		
	I don't usually think about what has happened during the day		
	I don't find it easy to say when I have done something well		
	I don't check my work for errors as I am working		

Classroom Audit through the SOWATT lens

S	• Engage in positive and meaningful relationships with every student	
	• Build a sense of community and belonging	
	• Provide opportunities to promote students' agency	
	• Establish daily routines to reduce stress and anxiety	
	• Establish clear and consistent behaviour expectations	
	• Praise the positive as much as possible	
	• Create an environment for students to feel safe to take a risk	
O	• Provide clear scope and sequence of transitions	
	• Give 'time alerts' for activities	
	• Shared resources need to be organised, labelled and easily accessible	
	• Provide opportunities to plan together – model the process	
	• Ensure students know what they need for each lesson	
W	• Create anchor charts of important information for students to refer to	
	• Be aware of the instructions you give, start simple and build in more steps and details	
	• Be aware of cognitive overload	
A	• Be aware of the classroom temperature – too warm and students are sleepy	
	• Be aware of the noise level – are there some quiet areas?	
	• Pay attention to the language in the classroom, what are you hearing/saying?	
	• Look around the room – what might distract students?	
T	• Change the physical layout from time to time to encourage children to be flexible	
	• Vary the routines from time to time, once students feel secure	
	• How are you showing you value curiosity?	
	• Provide choice and some open-ended activities	
T	• Make time for reflection during the day	
	• Check in with the students – ask them how they're going	
	• Ask students to explain their thinking – "What makes you say that?"	

Teacher checklist of student learning
(After Whitebread et al., 2009)

		Term 1	Term 2	Term 3	Term 4
	Initiates tasks without prompting				
	Uses previously taught strategies				
	Recovers from setbacks without giving up				
	Manages frustration or anxiety during learning				
	Works cooperatively with peers				
	Sets clear goals for the task				
	Plans steps before beginning a task				
	Is prepared for each lesson				
	Manages their time well on extended assignments				
	Written work is well presented				
	Follows instructions methodically				
	Builds on the ideas of others during discussions				
	Can speak about how they have done something, or what they have learned				
	Listens attentively to instructions				
	Stays focused for duration of task				
	Asks questions when unsure what to do				
	Listens respectfully to others				

		Term 1	Term 2	Term 3	Term 4
	Changes strategy if one is not working for them				
	Able to appreciate different viewpoints on a subject				
	Is aware of own strengths and weaknesses				
	Demonstrates understanding of task requirements				
	Can explain what strategies they are using				
	Knows their own strengths and weaknesses in learning				
	Monitors progress and seeks help appropriately				
	Verbalises what they are thinking during problem solving				
	Evaluates the effectiveness of the approach after completing the task				
Mindset	Shows confidence in their ability to succeed				
	Seeks feedback to improve				
	Accepts mistakes as part of learning				

Teaching SOWATT to primary students – sample activities

Circle-time activities

Examples of skill-reflection prompts:

S	• When have you acted without thinking? What happened? • What can you do next time to stay calm or pause first?
O	• Why is planning important? • How do you stay organised when working on something over an extended period of time?
W	• What helps you remember what to do? • What tricks do you use to stay on track?
A	• What distracts you most in class? • How do you bring your focus back?
T	• What do you do when your plan doesn't work? • Can you share a time you changed your thinking?
T	• How do you check your own learning? • What have you learned from a mistake recently?

Examples of closing circle questions:
- "Which SOWATT skill do you think is your super strength?"
- "Which one would you like to grow this week?"

Journalling

Invite students to create a small booklet or journal with a page for each SOWATT skill.

On each page they write or draw:
- What that skill means to them
- A time they used it
- Identify a goal to help you develop this skill

This can also become a year-/term-long reflection journal!

SOWATT skills map

Create a classroom chart with six sections – one for each SOWATT skill.

Throughout the week, students can write or draw examples of when they used that skill and add it to the wall.

This becomes a living bulletin board of executive function in action!

SOWATT scenario skits

In small groups, students act out everyday classroom situations where the SOWATT skills are needed.

Examples:

- A group project with no plan (**organisation**)
- A game where someone loses but bounces back (**self-regulation**)
- Getting stuck on a maths problem and trying new ways (**thinking flexibly**)

Then, pause and ask:

- "Which SOWATT skill could help here?"
- "What might you say/do?"

Design your own SOWATT superhero

Each student creates a character that represents one of the SOWATT skills.

Prompt:

- Draw your superhero.
- Name their skill and describe how they use it to help others.
- Share with the class or create a bulletin board titled 'Super Thinkers of Room ___'

Examples of 3 x 3 grid for retrieval practice

Forces and motion

What is a force?	Name three forces	What does gravity do?
Push or pull? (Give two examples)	What helps things move faster?	What makes things slow down?
How do we use force in sport?	What is friction?	Draw something moving and label the force

Class novel – *Charlotte's Web*

Who is Wilbur and what makes him special?	Describe Charlotte in three words	Where does the story take place?
What problem does Wilbur face?	What do the animals think about humans?	What did Charlotte write in her web?
Why is friendship important in the story?	How does Wilbur change by the end?	What message do you think the author wanted to share?

How to use it in class:

- **Independent retrieval:** See how many squares you can answer from memory.
- **Pair quiz:** One student picks a square, the other answers.
- **Whiteboard version:** Pick three random boxes to complete as a warm-up.
- **Exit ticket:** Complete three boxes before leaving the room.
- **Post-reading activity:** Great for checking comprehension and encouraging reflection.
- **Book club:** Use in small groups to spark discussion.
- **Creative extension:** Choose three squares and turn them into a comic strip or diary entry.

Group work self-assessment: Lower primary

Working together – self-assessment rubric			
How did I go?	😊 I did this well	😐 I did this a little	😟 I need help with this
I listened to my group			
I shared my ideas			
I took turns and was fair			
I helped my group			
I stayed on task			

Group work self-assessment rubric – collaboration and contribution: Upper primary

Criteria	4 – Excellent	3 – Good	2 – Developing	1 – Needs improvement
Participation	I was fully involved in all tasks and stayed on task.	I participated most of the time and usually stayed on task.	I sometimes joined in but got distracted or off task.	I rarely joined in or let others do most of the work.
Sharing ideas	I shared helpful ideas often and listened to others.	I shared ideas and listened to others most of the time.	I sometimes shared ideas or had trouble listening to others.	I didn't share much and often talked over others.
Teamwork	I encouraged others, helped when needed and solved problems calmly.	I worked well with most group members and was helpful.	I sometimes found it hard to work with others.	I argued or didn't cooperate with my group.
Responsibility	I completed my part on time and checked in with the group.	I completed most of my part and tried to be responsible.	I did some of my part but needed reminders.	I didn't complete my part or waited for others to do it.
Respect & communication	I used kind words, took turns and showed respect to everyone.	I was mostly respectful and spoke politely.	I was sometimes respectful but could have done better.	I was disrespectful or didn't listen to others.
Problem solving	I stayed calm and helped the group work through any problems.	I tried to solve problems fairly when they came up.	I had trouble solving problems without getting upset.	I gave up easily or made the problem worse.

Total score: _____ /24

Question matrix

	is/are/was	did/do	can/would	will	might
Who					
What					
Where					
When					
Why					
How					

Level 1 | Level 2 | Level 3 | Level 4

Examples of metacognitive prompts

Before learning. Help students activate their prior knowledge and think about strategies they might use	- "What is your goal?" - "What do you already know about this topic?" - "Have you done something like this before?" - "What might be tricky about this task?" - "What questions do you have before we begin?" - "How might you approach this task?" - "How will you know if you are on the right track?"
During learning. Encourage self-monitoring as they engage with tasks	- "How is it going so far?" - "What are you noticing?" - "Do you need to change your plan?" - "What can you do if you get stuck?" - "Is this strategy working for you?" - "What else could you try?" - "How confident are you that you understand the material?" - "Can you explain your thinking so far?"
After learning. Encourage reflection on their thinking and learning process	- "What worked well?" - "What was easy about this task? What was hard?" - "What strategies helped you succeed?" - "What would you do differently next time?" - "What helped you stay focused?" - "What was the most challenging, and how did you overcome it?"
As part of the above, provide Talk Stems to scaffold metacognitive thinking. These can be modelled by the teacher first	- "I'm thinking…" - "I'm wondering…" - "I'm noticing…" - "I'm picturing…" - "It reminds me of…" - "I figured out…" - "I just learned…"

Metacognitive prompts and questions for writing a persuasive speech

BEFORE WRITING – Planning my approach

"What's the purpose? What do I need to do before I start?"

- **What's the goal?**
  I need to convince my audience to agree with my point of view.
- **Who is my audience?**
  Are they students, teachers or a general public audience? That affects my tone and examples.
- **Do I understand the topic?**
  What do I already know? What more do I need to find out?
- **What's my main message?**
  What do I want my audience to believe, feel or do by the end?
- **What's my plan?**
  I'll brainstorm my main argument, come up with two to three supporting points and plan my intro and conclusion.

DURING WRITING – Monitoring my progress

"How's it going? Am I on track?"

- **Is my argument clear?**
  Does my opening clearly state my opinion?
- **Are my reasons strong and relevant?**
  Have I explained why my point makes sense, not just what I think?
- **Am I using persuasive techniques?**
  Have I used emotive language, rhetorical questions, repetition or facts?
- **Am I writing for my audience?**
  Am I using the right tone? Will this connect with the people listening?
- **What can I fix as I go?**
  Is a sentence too long? Is something off-topic? I can make small edits now.

AFTER WRITING – Reflecting and improving

"What worked well? What needs fixing?"

- **Does it persuade?**
  Would I be convinced by this? Why or why not?
- **Is my structure strong?**
  Intro with a hook, body with clear arguments and a powerful conclusion?
- **Is my language powerful?**
  Did I use strong vocabulary and persuasive devices effectively?
- **Did I meet the success criteria?**
  Let me check against the rubric or checklist.
- **What will I do differently next time?**
  Did I spend enough time planning? Should I ask a peer to give feedback?

Embedding metacognition

Exit tickets

- Keep them short.
- Where possible, ask open-ended questions.
- Make them relevant to the lesson objectives.
- Challenge students to synthesise what they have learned.
- Provide a safe and supportive environment for students to share their thoughts.
- Collect the tickets and use the information to inform your teaching.
- Consider using digital exit tickets for easier collection and feedback.

Short answer/prompt questions on learning

- "What was the most interesting thing we learned today?"
- "What was your favourite part of today's lesson?"
- "What did you find tricky about today's lesson?"
- "Draw a picture that shows what you learned today."
- "Write one thing you learned and one question you still have."
- "What would you do if you could go back and change something in today's lesson?"
- "Tell me about a time you used what we learned today."
- "What did you learn about yourself today?"

Short answer/prompt questions on confidence/mindset

- "How well do you feel you understood today's lesson?"
- "What is one thing you'd like me to explain more clearly?"
- "What was the most important thing you learned in today's class? Why is it important?"
- "How well did you work today on a scale of one to five? Describe why you feel this way."
- "How could the knowledge you learned today be used in the real world?"
- "What's one thing you want to practise again?"
- "What are you struggling to understand at the moment?"

www.ingramcontent.com/pod-product-compliance
Lightning Source LLC
Chambersburg PA
CBHW052032070526
44584CB00016B/2007